# LEAD, FOLLOW

## or Get Out of the Way!

*Daisy Hepburn*

**Regal Books**

A Division of GL Publications
Ventura, CA U.S.A.

**Other good reading:**
*The Measure of a Woman* by Gene A. Getz
*Yet Will I Trust Him* by Peg Rankin
*Glorify God and Enjoy Him Forever* by Peg Rankin

The foreign language publishing of all Regal books is under the direction of Gospel Literature International (GLINT). GLINT provides financial and technical help for the adaptation, translation and publishing of books for millions of people worldwide. For information regarding translation contact: GLINT, P.O. Box 6688, Ventura, California 93006.

Published by Regal Books
A Division of GL Publications
Ventura, California 93006
Printed in U.S.A.

**Library of Congress Cataloging in Publication Data**
Hepburn, Daisy.
    Lead, follow or get out of the way.

    Includes bibliographical references.
    1. Women—Conduct of life.    2. Women—Religious life.    I. Title.
BJ1610.H46          248.8'43              81-84568
ISBN 0-8037-0822-7                        AACR2

# CONTENTS

# Introduction

The 80s is the DECADE OF THE WOMAN.

There are more women in the ranks of the employed now than ever before, and the numbers grow daily. Women are becoming executives in corporations and presidents of colleges, airline pilots and attorneys, mayors of great cities and athletic achievers at every level. Women are being challenged to accept highly financed leadership training to improve their skills for this progressiveness.

I am beginning to be convinced that we have been *thrust* into these battles for "rights" and that we have lagged in assuming leadership responsibilities. What am I supposed to think about all of this change? What has it all to do with me? How should I react to this unexpected limelight? More important, what does Jesus say about *greatness* and *leadership*—not just to the women but to everyone?

"Whoever wants to become great among you must be your *servant*" (Matt. 20:26, italics added).

How does the role of servanthood fit with the new

roles women are assuming? Have we been too much influenced by the world's ideas of success and leadership?

Aggressiveness, a certain tinge of ruthlessness, and always selfishness are what I envision when I think of the woman leader for the 80s. Of course this is not necessarily so; the television screen filled with shouting, marching women contributes to that image. But the Bible teaches that God's idea of a leader—one who guides or conducts by showing the way (according to the dictionary)—is a *servant*. Servant-leadership for appropriate women's ministries is a desperate need for the 80s for the church of Jesus Christ!

It will probably require a whole change of mindset.

Perhaps we will have to study the Word, to discover new principles for leadership—to learn to *serve*, and therefore to influence and to guide.

Women in my age group—and let's not get too personal—the 40-60 age group, and even beyond are in *prime time*. We have just begun to recover from the shock of the "empty-nest syndrome" and we are more available for servant-leadership than ever before.

All sorts of changes have taken place in our home. My husband is happier with less food, believe it or not. It is easier for me to keep house now than it has ever been. We have a strange second car that we lovingly refer to as The Bomb, but nevertheless is acceptable if not always dependable transportation. There are so many things that I am free to do now that even three or four years ago I was not free to do.

It's *prime time* for us women, and surely God has the right to expect those of us who have spent years in being taught through marvelous Bible studies, inspirational pulpit teaching and a veritable avalanche of inspirational reading to begin to bear fruit through service.

It's *prime time*, and the local church can experience a new surge of vitality as God's women are willing to invest

## 6   *Lead, Follow or Get Out of the Way*

their strength and spiritual gifts in willing service, in *leadership*—based on the principles Jesus taught.

I want to help you make this decade of the 80s significant for service.

I want you to help too—so lead, follow or get out of the way!

# One

## How Would You Like to Be Introduced?

"How do you want to be introduced?" What a question! Dropping my eyes coyly, I mentioned a few little things she might want to say: wife, mother of two, washer of clothes, driver of car, regular church attender, etc. But, How would I *like* to be introduced?

"How about as an Olympic ski champion? Or the Pillsbury Bake-Off winner? Or Pulitzer Prize winner? Or Super Mom?" My imagination was running away with me. Wouldn't it be fun to be the great imposter for just a little while, or during *one* away-from-home circle meeting where I was speaking? I had heard over and over again introductions that made me feel singularly ordinary by comparison—and I dream of being introduced as somebody extra-ordinary!

My ordinariness is an embarrassment to me at times!

It was freezing cold when I pulled in to the parking lot and walked through the door of a local Christian radio station. Unaccustomed to being on the radio, the prospect of being interviewed held kind of a double fascination for me. It was only a 15-minute, Monday morning local program but I was delighted to be recorded on those marvelous ether airwaves and delighted at the fame that I was sure would result. Yes, there was a heady anticipation and excitement to the whole affair.

"I am Daisy Hepburn and I have an appointment with Kaaren," I said to the young woman at the switchboard.

"Just a moment, dear," she said, and she proceeded to call Kaaren. When Kaaren finally emerged from the "inner office" she proved to be one of those people who is entirely too good-looking for her own well-being! I was caught off guard to say the least. In a sweet, very sweet tone, she said, "Oh Daisy! I am so happy to meet you. Please just sit down and tell me all about yourself!" A leading question if I ever heard one.

"Well," I said, gulping, "what's to tell? We have two children, or they have us, actually—I have been married to the same man for nearly 30 years—we have moved 16 or 18 times and—and—" I just couldn't think of anything noteworthy to say. Finally I sighed, "I guess you could just say that the Lord Jesus has led us through *an adventure in the ordinary!*"

Kaaren's face lit up: "*An adventure in the ordinary*—it's a great phrase and we will use it on the air."

Before I could collect myself I was ushered into an inner sanctum, known "in the trade" as the taping studio, and given a seat behind a table. In front of me was a very large microphone. My eyes were drawn to the control booth where I saw a young man who appeared to be a life-size replica of Winnie the Pooh. Dudley began to signal with a smile and a series of gestures that it was time for us to begin. Kaaren listened for her cue as the music waned and said, "Good morning, ladies. We have with us today right here in our studio a lady who has lived through an *adventure in the ordinary!* Tell us about it, Daisy Hepburn!"

How can I tell you? I sat there and was struck dumb! I could not think of one single thing that was worth wafting out over those airwaves to the listening, waiting world. Not one thing of sufficient value to share in that moment.

An adventure in the ordinary! "Do tell us about it, Daisy!"

Well, I think I babbled on about my mother-in-law's coat and other tidbits that had little particular value. When Dudley finally signaled that we were through, all I wanted to do was get out of there. Why had Kaaren invited me? Never have I felt so *ordinary.*

Betty Carlson, in her little book, *Life Is Worth Living,* said it so well when she told of a wizened little elderly nun in Duluth giving a group of recent graduates some farewell words. With a wave, she challenged them, "Remember, girls, never die of ordinariness!"

I am so thankful that our God did not plan for us to die of ordinariness or anonymity, but has given us special gifts, special abilities and special adventures.

How do you want to be introduced?

*As an extra-ordinary WOMAN OF GOD.*

I would love to be introduced as a great woman leader—I can think of dozens of great women of God—wouldn't it be fun to be introduced as one of them? But I am old-shoe me. But just because I am rather ordinary by anyone's standard, doesn't mean that the Lord does not have a unique place for me to fill. More than that, the Word of God challenges us to be willing to become all that God has in mind for us to be. That goal is nothing less than *excellence—perfection,* conformed exquisitely to the image of the Son of God Himself. Ordinary? Not for a minute!

In a world where women are demanding their rights we find Scripture offering an alternative to this demand—accepting responsibility; and even further, living in submission to the plan of God for our lives and His shaping process until we become *great* through *servanthood.* How would I like to be introduced as a great servant of the living God! Now that's a definition of a leader; one that is antithetical to the world's idea.

Paul, in 2 Timothy 2 depicts a gallery of portraits of the multi-faceted leader. Each one has leadership characteristics and functions that provide a study in equipping us to be servant-leaders by God's design. Each portrait represents a practical application for creative service: the teacher must learn to speak creatively in front of a group with poise; the ranking soldier should learn to creatively recruit others; the athlete to creatively work with priorities and goals and coaching others, etc.

I think I would like to be introduced as any one of the models Paul describes. As a teacher (2 Tim. 2:2) who is poised, a transmitter of truth, who accepts the responsibility of teaching others; as a soldier (vv. 3,4), able to take orders without question, loyal, prepared. I would like to be a soldier who isn't necessarily always the first one in line for the furlough, but who is willing to put on the whole armor of God and to do battle with sin. As an athlete (v. 5), disciplined, continually practicing for the competition, having a goal worth striving for. An athlete who is running herself but is willing to set the pace to coach others. As a farmer (v. 6), patient, willing to risk everything for the sake of a productive harvest. A farmer who patiently, yet expectantly anticipates the harvest. As a workman (v. 15) who is industrious; who has a plan and works the plan. A workman who takes a holy pride in his craft. A workman who follows directions in order to build. As a vessel (vv. 20,21) without personality of its own, but cleansed, available to be filled, poured out and filled again. Or as a servant—*especially* a servant, who is a love slave of the Lord God. The Master is looking for servants willing to do His bidding with a glad heart.

Does this sound like a tall order? Even impossible? Settle it at the start: to be God's person—just like Jesus— being and doing all that God designed us to be and do— requires more than the raw materials we bring to the project. But that is why we need Jesus. Christ died for all our inadequacies and our weaknesses. What we must do is present ourselves as living sacrifices, holy (and wholly) to Him—it is only reasonable. We are not to settle down in our ordinariness, to be conformed to the mold of the apathetic world—even the world of Christians—but we are to prove what is the good and perfect will of God (see Rom. 12:1,2).

It is a wonderful invitation to the world's greatest come-as-you-are party! Accept it, dress in the righteousness of Jesus Christ and present yourself. God will transform you into His servant—a servant-teacher, a servant-soldier, a servant-athlete, a servant-farmer, a servant-workman, a servant-vessel or a great servant-leader.

Be filled with His Spirit and watch Him change you!

I don't remember where I first heard this statement, but it has stayed with me, and I give it to you: *God loves you just the way you are—but too much to leave you that way!*

# Two

# Equipped for Excellence

Let's make it a cheer—a challenge—and write it into our women's ministries' by-laws and constitution: *Equipping leaders is essential for an effective ministry.*

## Give Me an *E* for *Exceptional!*

If you have read this far and are still open to taking another step in becoming what the Lord wants you to be, if you have been willing to step out in faith, to learn how to better serve the Lord Jesus, you are Exceptional.

I am always amazed when anyone at all responds to a challenge to learn how to be a better servant! When I started teaching this course for women, and the tables would all be set up exceptionally, and the posters of these seven figures in 2 Timothy 2 would be in place, smiling on all who came through the door, my heart took a leap that anyone at all would come to hear or to learn! It isn't necessarily the most appealing idea in the world—the prospect of having more responsibility and more opportunity to keep "busy."

But we lay it right on the line at the outset: God will

take you at your word! If you are willing to invest your time and apply yourself to excellence in serving, He will find you work!

It is certainly more comfortable to attend conferences and retreats to be inspired (and I delight in attending and speaking to dozens of those) than to see yourself right there as the Master comes home to check on the stewardship of the servants to whom talents have been given. Remember what happened to those who had done well? Of course you do!

"You have been faithful with a few things; I will put you in charge of many things" (Matt. 25:21,23). They didn't get a vacation, not on your life! They were given more work, more responsibility, and yet, greater reward.

It is something like the picture of the vessel in 2 Timothy 2:20,21. There are lots of very nice vessels in a household but there are only a few that are set apart for special service. They are vessels unto honor—no, one step further than that: they are *chosen vessels*, cleansed, *excepted* from ordinary uses, set apart for temple service. The Scripture teaches that we can *choose* to be *chosen* vessels, having been cleansed and being cleansed continually by applying 1 John 1:9 and becoming available to God's highest and holiest purposes. *Exceptional*—by choice!

## Give Me an *E* for *Expectation!*

Let the Expectation of the provision for your equipping be from Him. Someone has said that the ability or equipping follows the commitment. I think I believe that!

I also believe that we have a tendency to rise to what is expected of us.

Rollie was a typically difficult junior high kid in our group of a dozen or so varied j-hi kids in the church. Being the sponsor, I had dreamed up a talent program for Sunday evening presentation. Not one of them was necessarily gifted, but most of the kids practiced at least an old piano recital piece or a magic trick, hoping for a revelation of spiritual truth in the sleight of hand. But Rollie just didn't have the gumption or grit to get his "talent" together.

I called him Sunday afternoon just to check. "What are you doing, Rollie?" I inquired. I heard a background whirring. Rollie answered, "I am making popovers."

"How about your talent for tonight's program? Have you decided what it is you want to do? We're counting on you!"

"Daisy, I don't have a talent."

"Rollie, bring all your stuff and show everybody how to make popovers! Be sure to bring some of your finished product because everyone will want a sample."

I guess I just wasn't prepared for Rollie. That night he moved into the church sanctuary—we had to use the sanctuary for the benefit of the pianists and organist in the group. Rollie set up his table, donned his chef's cap and stacked up the Tupperware bowls in order of use. Then he began, "Ladies and gentlemen, I am about to make popovers. I guess you could say it is a talent of mine. Actually, I didn't know it was my talent until Daisy called and told me so—"

What a compliment! Is it possible that God could use us in others' lives to call forth abilities and talents—equipping for service—that we don't even realize are there? Can we begin to *expect* that His Spirit within longs to respond to our *expectation* that He will give us what we need to "make the teaching about God our Savior attractive" (Titus 2:10)?

Emerson said, "Our chief want in life is someone to make us do what we can."

Kenneth Taylor, in *The Living Bible* has paraphrased three verses that fit right here: "O my soul, don't be discouraged. Don't be upset. *Expect God to act!*" (Ps. 42:11, italics added); "We confidently and joyfully look forward to actually becoming all that God has had in mind for us to be" (Rom. 5:2); "For I live in eager *expectation* and hope that I will never do anything that will cause me to be ashamed of myself but that I will always be ready to speak out boldly for Christ" (Phil. 1:20, italics added).

## Give Me an *E* for *Enthusiasm!*

The root of *enthusiasm* is *en theos*—"in god." Let's claim it as "in God"—caught up in God-ness. An attitude of being completely sold out, convinced and therefore convincing! This quality of being in God ought to be the hallmark of our life and service. Do not let familiarity or routine dull this most important quality in your leadership.

From a favorite book of mine:

Lord,
  it takes two hands to clap.
  It takes a total involvement—
  a caught-up-ness—
  to respond to thee.

Clapping is joy
  and response
  and approval
  and saying, "I'm with you.
    Amen!"
And it takes two hands to clap.
One hand behind me, holding back, won't do
it.

Clapping is enthusiasm.
  (Lord God, I cannot escape thee!
  Enthusiasm—en theos—possessed by
God!)
  enthusiasm, with a little e,

<br>

is a polite and brittle expression
of a shallow sanction.

Enthusiasm—possessed by thee?
Oh, may it be so!
May there be no withholdings.

Lord, possess my life.
Take these, my hands—
both of them.

Amen.[1]

"Serve the Lord enthusiastically" (Rom. 12:11, *TLB*).

### Give Me an *E* for *Example!*

Without a doubt our most important tool for leadership is example! It is Jesus' idea! Jesus could have said, "Do as I say!" Instead, our Lord said, "Do as I *do!*" (see John 13:15).

The apostle Paul could say, "[Follow] my example" (Phil. 3:17).

Most of the listeners squirmed a bit when the leader suggested that each of us make a list of our own traits, habits or characteristics that we wish our children would emulate! Perhaps we understand the power of our example but it is uncomfortable to think too much about it. But how can we pray that the Lord will guard and keep our children—and others within our influence—pure and holy, and that He will protect them from the evil influences of this world—unless we are wiling to set the *example* of holy living? Unless we are willing to say, "Do as I do!"

Have you heard about the young lady who was fixing her ham for Sunday dinner? Before she put the ham in the oven she cut off the end and threw it away, and then put the rest in the roasting pan. One of her guests observing her asked why she threw away that large piece.

"Oh," she said, "I always saw my mother do it this

way."

When she had the opportunity she decided to ask her mother; her mother then asked *her* mother why had she always thrown away the end of the ham?

"I don't know why *you* do it, but I had to because I never had a pan big enough!"

Is it time to check out your example to see how and what others follow?

This is a vitally important leadership principle. We must be willing to live so as to say, "Watch me, do as I do, and I will show you Christ's way. I am willing to be your example in service and in ministry." Philippians 3:17 says to follow my example. Can you accept this challenge to let the Spirit of God live His life through you so that you can, with a *holy* pride like Paul's, become a viable role model for your children, church, or community?

Cathy Meeks, the assistant dean of women at Mercer University at Macon, Georgia, in her book *I Want Somebody to Know My Name* writes of her childhood in a poverty-stricken home in the South. She came to Christ as a young girl and maintained her faith in spite of the extremely difficult circumstances in her home. Her childhood was scarred by the disdain for blacks in their community, her father's despair and hopelessness acted out in alcoholism, and her lack of guidance from a teacher or church. She says, "I remember searching throughout my teen years for a role model, and I could not find one. As I grew up and became a college student in the 60s, my life and goals were changed when I decided to *become* A ROLE MODEL!"[2]

Example is our most potent leadership tool. But it involves great risk. The one "up front," the chairman, the leader, is the risk taker, becoming vulnerable to criticism and evaluation. When the speaker speaks, all the others—the listeners—can decide to accept or reject, make out a grocery list, or take notes on the message—or even make a note to let the speaker know where she could get her hair done a bit more chicly. The saying: "To avoid criticism, do nothing, say nothing, be nothing" is true. But when the leadership opportunity arises, the challenge of the saying is inadequate to provide courage to *do something, say something or be something*.

But take heart, God will make of you a Proverbs 31 kind of woman if you will let Him, and a 2 Timothy 2 kind of servant-leader.

### Give Me an *E* for *Excellence!*

In an article entitled, "Excellence: The Christian Standard," Senator Mark Hatfield wrote, "Our first responsibility is to utilize and mobilize the resources, the capacity, the intellect, the drive, the ambitions and all that God has given us, and to use them to the fullest. That comes first in whatever endeavor to which we are committed."[3]

Former HEW secretary John W. Gardner once said, "I am concerned with the fate of excellence in our society. If a society holds conflicting views about excellence, or cannot rouse itself to the pursuit of excellence, the consequence will be felt in everything it undertakes."[4]

Excellence in our service; let it be our goal. We can get by, even acceptably, with mediocrity: "Let's not go to any trouble this time! Let's keep it really simple." Simplicity itself is desirable; complications occur without encouragement; but simplicity because of laziness is not a worthy goal. Remember that God's standard is excellence—perfection. His plan is for you to be conformed to the excellence of Jesus Christ. And in Him there is nothing mediocre.

Paul was in pursuit of excellence. If ever there was anyone who could have sat back resting on his qualifications, and who did not get ruffled even after his encounter with the living God, it was Paul. Philippians 3 is a chronicle of his quest for excellence: "But whatever was to my profit I now consider loss for the sake of Christ.

What is more, I consider everything a loss compared to the surpassing greatness of knowing Christ Jesus my Lord, for whose sake I have lost all things. I consider them rubbish that I may gain Christ" (vv. 7,8).

Philippians 3 is Paul's priority chapter in his pursuit of excellence. The first step in his pursuit was to have a personal knowledge of Christ (vv. 7,10). That is number 1— *the goal*!

Second *his motivation*, verses 10-12, was that he aspired to actually become like Christ. That possibility became the motivation for all he did.

Third, he aggressively pursued excellence: "Forgetting what is behind and straining toward what is ahead, I press on toward the goal" (vv. 13,14).

Leroy Eims, in his book *Be the Leader You Were Meant to Be* says that God works in our lives in at least seven ways to bring about a spirit of excellence:

1. By helping us realize our own weakness—2 Corinthians 12:9;

2. Through the prayers of others—Colossians 4:12;

3. Through someone sharing the Word with us—1 Thessalonians 3:10;

4. As we study the Bible for ourselves—2 Timothy 3:16,17;

5. Through suffering—1 Peter 5:10;

6. By giving us a hunger for holiness—2 Corinthians 7:1;

7. Through a desire to have the fruit of our lives brought to perfection—Luke 8:15.

"Some words of caution need to be sounded at this point. First, we need to examine our motivation. Excellence for its own sake is not our standard, but excellence for Christ's sake."[5]

School was fun for me—especially grammar school. Report card time held not much threat for me. But in spite of how well I did in grades, my dad's reaction was always the same: That and better will do! It would run through my head; Dad said it often—not just for report cards. He challenged his five daughters with a word of acceptance first, then a challenge to do better. I have been told that William Booth, the founder of the Salvation Army inspired and challenged his "disciples" with those words and Dad just picked up on the theme. But it worked! Daddy built strongly on the foundation of acceptance—but no status quo sufficed for long.

A couplet comes to mind and I don't even remember where I first heard it:

Good, better, best, never let it rest
Until your good is better and your better—best!

**Notes**

1. Jo Carr and Imogene Sorley, *Bless This Mess* (New York: Pillar Books, 1969), p. 64.
2. Cathy Meeks, *I Want Somebody to Know My Name* (Nashville: Thomas Nelson, Inc., 1978).
3. Mark Hatfield, "Excellence: The Christian Standard," *World Aflame*, April 1978, p. 5
4. John W. Gardner, Ibid.
5. Leroy Eims, *Be the Leader You Were Meant to Be* (Wheaton, IL: Victor Books, 1975), p. 50.

## Three

# The Teacher

"You then, my son, be strong in the grace that is in Christ Jesus. And the things you have heard me say in the presence of many witnesses entrust to reliable men who will also be qualified to teach others" (2 Tim. 2:1,2).

You, there, *be strong*, and *teach*! Two special requirements for being a teacher in the Saviour's school: Teach others and Teach truth! Whether we like it or not we are teachers. The choice is ours as to what we teach. When I remember those who have been my teachers I often find it difficult to put my finger on exactly what information I have gleaned because the *person* who was my teacher spoke so much louder than did his or her words.

I had a junior high teacher like that. She made us want to come to school! First, she always looked so nice. As I think of it now, there was nothing unusual about her clothes or her hairdo, but I do have a clear image that she was so well-groomed.

She had a kind of dignity about her that seemed to let us know that she was in charge and knew exactly what she would do next. Fred was always a problem to her, but she patiently accepted his tardiness, his messiness, his laziness about his homework, and determined to help Fred catch up so he could be promoted.

Miss DiVincenzo was the recipient of valentines and apples, notes and wild flowers—how we looked for ways to please her. She was a teacher who made us want to learn because she made it seem so very important—just by being who she was.

Dr. Clyde Narramore believes that it is the right of every child to receive some encouragement every day. One teacher, Miss Johnson, accepted his challenge to do just that for students within her influence. She mimeographed the list of students in her class and, each day, checked the name of each student as she took opportunity to encourage him or her. One day one of her students, Vincent, had been incorrigible—nothing about his person or behavior allowed for encouragement! As the final bell rang, signaling that she wouldn't see the children until the next day, Miss Johnson remembered her commitment to encouragement; she took a deep breath, patted Vincent as he left the room, and said, "Vincent, you certainly were *vital* today!"

## Be a Teacher Who Encourages!

My first-grader nephew Frankie told his mom, as she was getting him ready for school, to put his shoes on the wrong feet. "Whatever for?" she asked, as he kicked off his oxfords to the floor.

"Because—when I get to school my teacher will say, 'Frankie, you have your shoes on the wrong feet again!' and then she will sit me down and fix them—and Mom, I like the way she *smells!*"

"But thanks be to God! For through what Christ has done, he has triumphed over us so that now wherever we go he uses us to tell others about the Lord and to spread the Gospel like a sweet perfume. As far as God is concerned there is a sweet, wholesome fragrance in our lives.

It is the fragrance of Christ within us, an aroma to both the saved and the unsaved all around us. To those who are not being saved, we seem a fearful smell of death and doom, while to those who know Christ we are a life-giving perfume. But who is adequate for such a task as this? Only those who, like ourselves, are men of integrity, sent by God, speaking with Christ's power, with God's eye upon us" (2 Cor. 2:14-17, *TLB*).

Be a teacher with the sweet fragrance of Christ about your life.

If the qualification of the 2 Timothy 2 teacher is that we are transmitters of truth, it will do us well, teacher-leaders, to consider what is being transmitted through our lives.

Miss Hamel was my Sunday School teacher when I was just a little girl. My sisters and I attended the Christian and Missionary Alliance Sunday School near Times Square in New York City. Our parents were in the Salvation Army and our dad directed a center for alcoholics in "hell's kitchen" not far from where the Alliance church was located.

Miss Hamel was a maiden lady who had a desire to transmit truth to the four or five of us who sat under her tutelage. It was back in those old days when flannelgraph was just being introduced as the ultimate visual aid. But Miss Hamel hadn't gotten that message yet, and she was confident that she could get the truth of the Word into our mind without any new-fangled aids. And she did! We were assigned a certain number of verses each week, and we competed and won bookmarks and colored buttons and especially her approval as we memorized and memorized.

She knew the Word could be depended upon to produce fruit in our lives and that it was not necessary that we understand all that the Beatitudes meant before we learned them, or the first Psalm, or the one-hundredth Psalm, or John 1, and on and on and on. Now that I think about it, most of the Scripture I now know by heart I learned before I was 12 years old! And if I had waited until I understood it, I wouldn't have it now!

## Be a Transmitter of Truth!

Edith Schaeffer said in her book, *What Is a Family?*, that home is the place where truth is transmitted, or ought to be. We are teachers in our own homes, transmitting the truth of the gospel in authentic living from one generation to another. In the first chapter of 2 Timothy we get just a glimpse into Timothy's home, and again in Acts 16. Imagine Paul knocking on the door of that little home and inquiring within, "Is there someone here who has been made ready, has been taught to serve the Lord here?" Grandma Lois and Mother Eunice smile and say, "Here he is! A graduate of the school of homemade Christian education! Timothy is ready to go with you!"

I believe I have a knack with kids, or at least I used to think so. We were fresh and green to the staff of a children's home in northern California. One of my choicest assignments was to create a Sunday evening worship service for the kids from 7 to 11 years old. This unwieldy group of about 50 met in a room we liked to call the library. These were kids from all sorts of backgrounds, all sorts of homes, foster homes, and juvenile halls, mostly wards of the court in the many counties of California. Every Sunday evening I would enlist a pianist from the staff and we would have a go at it. A good share of the kids had never been to Sunday School, much less to Sunday evening services; but dressed in the whole armor of God we went to the fray.

I remember that this particular evening I was teaching the children about prayer. "Now we are going to pray," I said. But in order to involve them I suggested that maybe they could give us some prayer requests, some special things they thought we ought to pray about.

Many hands shot up and I called on them one at a

time and we made our list.

"Margie's foster mother lost a check"; "Jim was really missing his dog"; "Felix had all his week's allowance stolen," and on and on we went.

When I finally had to call a halt to all we were about to take to the Lord I asked, while the piano was being played softly, if we could bow our heads and spend just a moment in silent prayer. I smiled in my own super-spiritual way—I was actually encouraging this amazing collection of kids in the fine art of prayer. I had my eyes closed, savoring the silence reverently. Yet inside I had this awful desire to peek. Finally that desire got the best of me and, with one eye open, I saw Darryl way in the back raise his hand.

I knew he was going to say something which was sure to contribute to the sweet spirit in that place so I inquired as to what it was he wanted. From the back of the room he yelled, "Hey, Daisy, you're all open in front." Sometimes even our best efforts seem to be thwarted. I buttoned my blouse and carried on.

Then there was Bobby, just eight years old. Bobby came to church every Sunday night waiting for the opportunity to share his Scripture verse. I would say, "Well, kids, remember we are all learning our verses. Isn't there someone here who has a special verse you have learned this week?"

Actually it was surprising that I even expected any of the kids to stop their fussing and feuding and eating and running and reading long enough to learn a Scripture verse, but Bobby raised his hand every Sunday night.

"Yes, Bobby, let's hear from you."

"Jesus said, don't say shut up to the cottage mother."

"Well, Bobby, that is certainly a good and important thought, but I don't think it is right from the Bible."

"Jesus said, don't take all the ham first."

"Jesus said, quit stealing your friend's allowance."

Little by little, I tried to feed in the fact that just to put

"Jesus said" in front of a good thought did not make it the inerrant Word of God. Bobby tried so hard to do what I find myself trying to do—add authority to my life by claiming all my behavior is guided by the Lord Jesus. Not too bad an idea after all, is it?

### Be a Teacher-Leader Who Teaches Others!

A Titus 2 directive says that older women are to teach the younger women to be quiet and respectful in everything they do. They must not go around speaking evil of others, they must not be heavy drinkers, they should be teachers of goodness. These older women must train the younger women to live quietly, to love their husbands and their children and be sensible and clean minded. They should be pure, keepers at home, good, obedient to their own husbands, that the Word of God be not blasphemed.

There is a marvelous church in southern California that has a unique women's ministry. I asked the pastor of this growing church, known for its teaching ministry, what part the women played to account for its phenomenal growth. He said one of the most effective is called Keepers-at-Home. Several older women invite four or five younger women to their homes where they spend a morning or an afternoon learning canning or quilting or breadmaking or ways to have a family altar with active children. Then once a quarter the younger women sponsor a luncheon at the church for the ladies who had been willing to teach. They all "dress up and have someplace to go!"

It is refreshing to realize that there are churches, alive and growing, where the middle-aged and older women are challenged to teach the younger women, and in such creative ways. Is your church ready for a Keepers-at-Home ministry?

Malettor Cross is a strong, dignified black mother of 11 children from Detroit, Michigan. Her eyes glistened

with enthusiasm and zeal as she shared with me the burden on her heart for black women.

"The need is overwhelming for gut-level Bible teaching. The Word of God has not been taught to the blacks
enough to bring about changed lives. The black community has been exploited by its own people and others.
That is not to say that God has not raised up some fine,
well-educated black teachers and preachers. But there
have been so may others who have taught the Word
when it has benefited *them*, for their *own* support, and
not for the benefit of the hearer."[1]

Mrs. Cross was now into her element. This was the
passion of her heart—to *teach teachers*! She was talking
so fast and vibrantly, I had a hard time keeping up—

"Yes, Daisy, that is what it is all about! In our conferences where we are trying to get black women to teach
other black women, we want to scratch where it itches.
We want to teach women not only how to be Christians,
but how to *live as Christians*. ['Just as you received Christ
Jesus as Lord, continue to live in him' (Col. 2:6).]

"This is my excitement now. I have two classes, one
to train children's teachers, and one to train Bible class
instructors. I have let all my ladies know that they are
expected to go out and teach others. I tell them to acti-
vate 2 Timothy 2:2—to go and teach others."

Malettor went on to say that she felt that the government has been so careful in recent years to provide
blacks with opportunity for higher education, and that
thousands are graduating from colleges and universities
each year, schooled in humanistic philosophies. Her
heart's cry is that the church of Jesus Christ would soon
catch up—women teaching other women and our young
people in the principles of the changeless Word of God.

## Effective Teaching Methods

Let's consider some of the teaching methods Jesus
has used.

*Visual tool*—In John 8, Jesus was outside the Temple and a group of leaders and Pharisees put an adulteress on display in ridicule. " 'Teacher,' they said to Jesus, 'this woman was caught in the very act of adultery. Moses' law says to kill her. What about it?' " (John 8:4, *TLB*).

Silently, yet most eloquently, Jesus stooped and wrote in the sand. How our imaginations have wondered what He wrote! Whatever it was, there was a reaction, then pressure to verbalize His answer so that they could criticize.

"Go ahead and throw stones at her—but let the one who is without sin cast the first stone!" (see v. 7).

The Jewish leaders and others in the crowd left one by one as Jesus stooped again and wrote silently. It is apparent that whatever He wrote packed the punch necessary to convict and disperse the crowd.

Barbara Johnson is the mother of a homosexual, and her book *Where Does a Mother Go to Resign?* is priceless. She has a wit and humor that is a unique gift and a useful teaching tool. I love to share a quote from her book: "I'm always in the midst of an energy crisis and an identity crisis at the same time. I don't know who I am, but I am too tired to find out!"[2]

She gave me a stone one day last fall. On it are painted some flowers and the words: DAISY'S FIRST STONE. As she presented it to me she said, "Daisy, you must hang onto this. Actually, you might try to throw it some time, but you will probably never be able to follow through. It is a reminder of Jesus' words—that only those who are without sin can throw the first stone. Those of us who carry a first stone have grown to realize that none of us is perfect yet—and we just have to use our stones as paper weights, or as kitchen windowsill reminders."

What a visual tool for combating the spirit of criticism!

In Matthew 22:15-22 Jesus spoke again to leaders. They tried to trap Him and trick Him into a conversation concerning the duty of a taxpayer. Jesus met them on their ground and asked them to show Him a coin—right out of their own pocket. A teaching tool and a principle of communication: *meet your audience on their territory.* Do not speak to a group of financiers on agriculture or to a group of single women on child rearing.

*Discussion*—In John 4 Jesus met the woman of Samaria at Sychar's Well. The conversation was like a seesaw. The lady changed the subject just as often as she could, and Jesus skillfully kept up with her. Topics ranged from racial prejudice to the history of Israel, to her marital status, to places of worship, and each time Jesus came closer to accomplishing His purposes in the encounter. Again, He used visual aids—the well, the water and the water pot and "many of the Samaritans from that town believed in him because of the woman's testimony" (John 4:39).

*Demonstration*—In John 13, Jesus was in the upper room with His disciples and He illustrated how they were to serve. He could have simply told them but instead He filled a basin with water and, with a towel, knelt down in front of each of them and washed their feet. Do you think they ever forgot Christ's example in living demonstration of how to?

*Field trip*—A trip to the Temple to observe a widow giving all she had in the offering served to illustrate, and then confirm, the spirit in which each of us is to give. He could have lectured on stewardship and invited pledges; instead He used a field trip. He only needed to summarize His lesson for maximum effectiveness.

*Projects*—After teaching the disciples, Jesus sent them out two by two to practice. He knew that students learn by doing and He sent them to see people, to listen to them, to share their experiences, and to share the message of salvation.

*Drama*—And what a drama was played out in the Temple as Jesus made a whip and drove out the money changers!

Teacher, observe the Master Teacher using distractions and turning them into lessons about sowing seeds and harvesting crops, using whatever was at hand as visual tools in the hands of the Master Workman.

### The ABCs of Public Speaking

The teacher-leader, or servant-teacher, must be poised in front of a group. This is the leadership characteristic we will consider now.

You are invited to make a speech or give a devotion or share your testimony—and you have several choices: (1) decline and leave town; (2) accept and play hookey and find a substitute to take your place; (3) accept and cram until your nerves are standing on end and your family considers going on strike; (4) order a film; (5) accept and carefully develop a lesson plan.

Assuming you have settled on option #5, sharpen your pencil and do your homework. Following are some basic ABCs.

A—*Accept the challenge* and presume upon the Lord's enabling to communicate through you. "I can do everything through him who gives me strength" (Phil. 4:13).

An *Awareness of time* allotted will be appreciated by everyone.

*Appropriateness* in dress is key—if in doubt, ask. Wear something you have worn before and are comfortable in. Wear a color that flatters you and makes a bold statement. Do not wear chains or jewelry that will distract. A skirt is *always* appropriate, though pants and pantsuits are not always so. Wear a long skirt if you are comfortable in one. Be certain that your clothes are not too tight for you.

Now I am a tall woman and enjoy wearing long skirts when I speak. (I think I feel that it is a good way to cover up runs in my stockings!) I always wear a daisy—usually a pin—but I have a navy blue sweater with embroidered daisies on it; it makes a statement! A yellow blouse with a long tie bow goes well under it and the bow looks good filling in the v-neck of the sweater.

No one in the room will ever forget a night service at a large Winning Women Retreat in Florida. I stepped to the pulpit and, after a few opening remarks, launched the main part of the message. Then I led the women to a portion of Scripture. I leaned over and picked up my bifocals (the better to see the words with, my dear), and lifted the glasses to my waiting eyes and nose. Inadvertently (how else?) I brought the long yellow ends of the tie with them! I couldn't see! The tie was making a blindfold of my bifocals! When I realized that the lights had not gone out and that the trouble was with me and my glasses, I wanted to have the platform open up and swallow me. The ladies were by that time laughing uproariously—and it was not a humorous part of the message. What poise I produced under that incredible pressure! Pulling myself together I didn't even refer to it, but moved right along. None of us will ever forget it, however!

B—*Be Yourself.* You are unique and no one will communicate just like you. Unique does not even take an adjective; you are not very unique, or almost unique, or less or more unique—you have a style and message all your own. Let the Lord use the you that you are.

*Be prepared.* Of course you will have all your thoughts in order, but take the time *before* the meeting begins to check the lectern and microphone. It is distracting and time-consuming to have to work with these arrangements during the gathering.

*Be careful* to eat lightly, if at all, before speaking. (This one makes me chuckle a little because I guess I eat everything put in front of me, at any time—and mostly out of nervousness!)

C—*Confidently communicate.* If you have prepared, and prayed that the Lord would communicate His message through you—even if it is only an announcement or an introduction of another speaker—be confident that *He will*. Do your part in preparation, and expect that God will do His. The most difficult part of your message is to leave the results with Him.

*Cut out fillers*—ah, er, um (and others!) Practicing with a tape recorder will reveal to you these weaknesses which you can correct with more practice.

*Cultivate an audience rapport* and make eye contact with two or three friendly faces right away. I can almost always pick out of an audience those who have been in front of a group before. Can you imagine how? You are right! They are the ones who are making eye contact with me, smiling their support and paying attention. Anyone who has been there, who has taken the risk to be "on display" sharing thoughts and information for consideration and evaluation, are your friends. Make eye contact with them.

*Cards are good for notes*. Don't use large sheets of paper or pages from a loose-leaf notebook.

D—*Don't read your speech*. All flexibility is lost and you often lose your audience if you resort to reading what you have carefully prepared.

*Don't grasp the lectern*. Stand tall and straight.

E—*Exercise ahead of time* by giving your speech in a mirror to yourself, or to your family. They will probably give you criticism.

*Excuses or apologies are a no-no*. Do not bore your audience with the reasons you are not prepared or doing better or unqualified or any problems relating to the meeting, etc., etc. This is an unprofessional defense mechanism. Perhaps we hope to get the sympathy of the hearers; instead we launch our speech with a negative distraction and we reveal our inadequacy. They will notice it soon enough!

*Enthusiasm* in your voice inflections will enhance your speech; listening to a tape of your speech will help you to know how you are doing.

## Listener's Laws for Speech Organization

The following four laws can apply to letters, news copy, sales presentations, or your personal testimony.

*Wake up!* Begin your talk by assuming that your audience is asleep and needs to be wakened. Don't count on the fact that they are waiting eagerly for what you are about to say. Imagine your listeners as bored—and about to register a loud HO-HUM!

*Why?* Be ready to build a bridge with your second thought. Convey right away that your listener is involved in some way with the message content. Why are you telling *them*? It is because their lives are affected in some way—and let them be able to identify the relevancy.

*Watch!* This is a demand of the listener, the for-instance, the show me! As the examples are stated, make sure they are presented in good order, and actually illustrate your points—interesting, humorous, personal, historical, biblical—the list can go on indefinitely. Make notes of stories, signs along the highway, or other resources for illustrations for your speeches.

*So what?* Now is the time to ask for specific action. Make it perfectly clear what action or response you expect from the audience. *Stand! Join! Contribute! Buy! Write!* Your closing statements must summarize and challenge and tie up loose ends.

It is good practice to prepare a three-minute speech, or about 250 words. Your own testimony or a brief segment of your own story is a good place to begin. And remember it is far more difficult to say something with purpose and power in three minutes than it is to prepare a half hour or an hour's presentation. You must be very selective, and you will do well to adhere to the four steps listed: Wake up! Why? Watch! and So what?

## Care and Feeding of Speakers

Now that you are launched with confidence to follow through on open doors of opportunity in speaking pub-

licly, let me share a homework checklist for speakers—
their care and feeding. If you are responsible for contacting speakers and developing programs for your women's
organization, learn to do it with grace.

1. Develop an acquaintance with potential speakers
and their ministries.

2. Title a file folder RESOURCE PEOPLE and collect
names, addresses, phone numbers, and brochures of
speakers.

3. When considering a speaker it is helpful to listen to
a tape or attend a meeting where the person is speaking.

4. When *contacting* the speaker, remember:
   a. state clearly the purpose of the gathering
   b. identify the group or church making the
      request
   c. state time, place and date of meeting
   d. discuss the honorarium—20¢ a mile is
      "going rate" for automobile travel; air
      fares are complicated and it is perhaps a
      good idea to check on possible air travel
      for economy before the speaker is con-
      tacted.

5. And—HERE SHE IS! Just introduce the speaker.
   a. Don't attempt a biography, just a few well-
      prepared sentences.
   b. Don't wait until the speaker arrives to find
      out about her. The hostess will be able to
      give you some details because of her con-
      tacts.
   c. A long introduction is as inappropriate as a
      too-short one: "I don't know much about
      Mrs. _____, so we will let her tell us
      about herself."

It has only happened twice but, as far as I am concerned, twice is too often! I had a morning appointment
and felt rather proud that I was clever enough to work

two activities—the coffee appointment with a lady who needed a broad shoulder to lean on for an hour or so, and the spring luncheon planned by a Methodist church in a suburb. It was April in Minneapolis, and I set out with spring in my step.

Excusing myself from the coffee meeting I hurried (by now I was running too close to the luncheon time) and parked in the Methodist church lot. Rushing in, I said to the lady in the cloakroom—the one I was sure had been sent out to wait for the tardy speaker—that I was Daisy Hepburn, and gave her my regrets. She looked quizzically, but asked me to follow her. Hardly waiting for her, much less following her, I dashed up behind the speaker's table and presented myself—hopefully in time for the buffet line. The chairman swung around as she heard me and looked me square in the eye and said, "You're for May!" Without stopping for lunch—without stopping for *anything*—I got out of there.

When I had to have a rerun the next month, I just entered as cooly as if nothing had happened at all!

It is such a good idea to call the speaker a day or two ahead of time to make certain that calendars are, in fact, coordinated!

We have really given up presenting programs for Sweetheart Banquets. Actually we gave them up a few years ago, and I think it was right after our experience with the Baptists at the Swiss Chalet Restaurant.

We arrived in plenty of time, with a car loaded with guitar, slide projector (for an audio-visual musical presentation) and even a cardboard bicycle-built-for-two. We went into the banquet room where the employees were arranging and setting tables. David kind of snapped his fingers and got the attention of the young man moving chairs. "Will you please move the piano over here, and then find me an extension cord so that I can set up this projector, and, and. . . ." There seemed to be a hesitancy, and we began to wonder if good help was available at all anymore!

The clock said 6:30, and there didn't seem to be a Baptist in sight! Finally I had the nerve to inquire, "Isn't this banquet set for 6:45? Where do you think the folks are with the flowers and programs?"

The waitress went back to the office, and returned to say, "This is an office party, and it is scheduled for 7:30. The *manager of Woolworth's* will be here by 7:00 to finalize the arrangements."

The date for the Baptist banquet was *February* 28, not *January* 28! This time, dressed to our teeth, we stayed for supper anyway! We were the most outstandingly attired but most thoroughly embarrassed pair eating in that cafeteria that evening!

Be a servant-teacher who is poised and prepared to speak.

## Notes

1. Daisy Hepburn, *Why Doesn't Somebody Do Something?* (Wheaton, IL: Victor Books, 1980).
2. Barbara Johnson, *Where Does a Mother Go to Resign?* (Minneapolis: Bethany Fellowship, Inc., 1979).

# Four

## The Soldier

"Endure hardship with us like a good soldier of Christ Jesus. No one serving as a soldier gets involved in civilian affairs—he wants to please his commanding officer" (2 Tim. 2:3,4).

The soldier who has willingly enlisted must be prepared for battle. Somehow, the idea of fighting from a foxhole has little attraction for me! The Scripture teaches that we Christian soldiers must be on front-line duty against spiritual enemies. "Put on the full armor of God, . . . so that you may be able to stand firm! Having done all!" (see Eph. 6:13).

Analyzing my Christian soldiering I discover the role of home-front recruiter to be comfortable, certainly more appealing than flapping about in boots and helmet in the infantry. As a matter of fact, I can imagine my continual opting for furloughs and R and Rs, not necessarily wanting a discharge, but neither wanting the risk of being wounded!

*Back to the basics!* Another go-round at basic training, that's what I really need. A refresher course in following the leader, personal disciplines, ready obedience, survival in stress, care of equipment and weapons is offered in the Word of God for those who have made a do-or-die commitment to the Commander-in-Chief.

There is not much call for generals in Scripture—God makes those selections. Soldier-servants, soldier-leaders, you come and volunteer to follow, and be so convinced of the cause that your life and attitude will quite naturally recruit others.

While responsible for a senior high week at Bible camp, I got the idea to supply our eager campers with a good stiff lesson in a week of "Basic Training for the Lord's Army."

"It will never work! You will never get high school kids to cooperate!" I had heard that "word of encouragement" year after year as we put many, many weeks of creative camping together for kids of all ages. But it did work! A leadership principle—at least one I am convinced of—is *you can get anybody to do almost anything if you are convinced yourself* and willing to let your sanctified imagination out of the cage (in this case, the *brig*).

(Can I put a whole paragraph in parentheses? Here goes: Remember when we talked about *enthusiasm* a chapter or two ago? Here it is again. It is almost frightening to see how enthusiastic leadership can mold and motivate a group. It is a tool often used destructively. We have witnessed riots, mob scenes, panic in crisis—whole groups of people swayed by the action or reaction or word of one person. As Christian soldiers let us use this important leadership advantage to motivate, to encourage, and to lead on to prove the principles of the Word of God into commitment to Him.)

Back to camp—

"Yes, Mrs. Hepburn, I do have a few minutes available. Why don't you come on over to Camp Ripley this morning?" As I hung up the phone, I squealed in delight. The colonel, the ranking officer at one of the Midwest's largest National Guard encampments, had listened to my idea and certainly sounded ready to cooperate. Maybe he hadn't heard me correctly, but I ran to the car and decided to find out face-to-face.

"Colonel, we have about 150 high school young people coming to camp next week, and we need some 'local color' to add to our theme of 'Basic Training for the Lord's Army.' " About that time I was sure he was thinking of lending me a parachute or a mess kit for an object lesson. But I had far more than that in mind.

"Is there a possibility of your sending over a tank or two, or a platoon of National Guardsmen, or maybe—" As the colonel's eyes widened he pushed his chair back from the desk and took a pencil in hand. Surprise of all surprises, he made some notes, then picked up the telephone. Summoning one of his aides he gave instructions to do "something for Mrs. Hepburn."

That something turned out to be: five major National Guard vehicles driving down the dirt road on the opening night of camp—23 miles to Lake Beauty! The National Guardsmen took our "inductees" on rides on the amphibian, the jeep, the derrick, and the half-ton. The guardsmen played a wild game of softball with our campers. I nearly invited them to stay for supper in the mess hall but was checked just in time. It was clear that they were enjoying the girls—a bit too much.

On Thursday morning, after a middle-of-the-night air raid drill and dawn calisthenics, we got an *alert* to go to the field! Colonel Phillips hadn't failed in even *one* respect. The helicopter came into sight and then hovered right over our "army." Then it landed right on the ball field! Out stepped the colonel with some recruiting posters under his arm. He knew a golden opportunity when he saw one; we had a whole bunch of very available high school seniors who were already in basic training!

With the staff in "fatigues," and the many recruiting

posters with Uncle Sam pointing his finger at passersby, it
was an unforgettable week. Each cabin "company" was
charged with the responsibility—from the Word of God—
to support their comrades in the battle. Unforgettable!
And *strenuous!* How I wish you could have seen those
kids. . . . "Let's have another rousing chorus of 'I May
Never March in the Infantry!' " And they sang!

## A Mighty Army

It will take more than a week of Bible camp to get us
spiritually ready, equipped and disciplined to face the
enemy.

Christ's soldier is committed to the Commander and
does not get tied up in worldly affairs. The soldier-leader
is single-minded, willing to be trained to instant obedience, and willing to forego even many *good* things in
order to please the Commander, the One who has chosen him to be a soldier.

In your ministry do you find it is hard to identify the
*soldiers?* Worldliness is almost an outmoded word. My
dad used to say to us, when we dared to put on a little lipstick or even earrings, "Oh my girls, you look too
worldly!" Both by demand and desire I wanted to please
my dad, and it took some time before I even asked per-
mission to wear lipstick. The price of his disapproval was
too high to pay!

Set-apartness, separation from the world—a distinc-
tiveness about those in the service of the Lord—is harder
to find now than it used to be. The enemy of our souls,
our homes, our families, our nation is not asleep. We will
be a more effective "army" if we are willing to be identified, both in attitude and action, as prepared to do battle
with sin.

Someone, a very long time ago, prepared the following article. It really should be read with a background of
brass band music playing "Onward Christian Soldiers."

"Last Sunday our pastor asked Jimmy Mitchell, just

back from two years at the front lines, if he'd be guest speaker at our church. Jimmy refused at first. Then, with a funny light in his eye, he said he would if the congregation sang 'Onward Christian Soldiers' just before he began. So we gave forth with the song, and Jimmy waded in. This is what he said:

'You have been singing, "Like a mighty army moves the church of God." That might have been all right once. The trouble now is that about ten million men know exactly how an army moves and it doesn't move the way a lot of you folks in our church do. Suppose the army accepted the lame excuses that many of you think are good enough to serve as alibis for not attending church.

'Imagine this, if you can. Reveille 7 a.m. Squads on the parade ground. This sergeant barks out, "Count fours. One! Two! Three! Number four missing. Where's Private Smith?"

' "Oh," pipes up a chap by the vacant place, "Smith was out late last night and needed the sleep. He said he would be with you in spirit."

' "That's fine," says the sergeant. "Remember me to him! Where's Brown?"

' "Oh" puts in another chap, "he's playing golf. He gets only one day a week for recreation, you know."

' "Sure, sure," the sergeant cheerfully answers. "Hope he has a good game. Where's Robinson?"

' "Robinson," explains a buddy, "is sorry not to greet you in person, but he is entertaining guests today. Besides, he was at drill last week."

' "Thank you," says the sergeant, smiling. "Tell him he's welcome any time he is able to drop in."

'Did any conversation like that ever happen in

the army? Don't make me laugh. Yet you hear stuff like that every week in the church, and said with a straight face, too.

'  "Like a Mighty Army!" If our church really moved like a mighty army, a lot of you folks would be court-martialed!' "[1]

> Like a mighty army
> Moves the Church of God;
> Brothers (and sisters), we are treading
> Where the saints have trod;
> We are not divided, all one body we;
> One in hope and doctrine, one in
> charity![2]

As the strains of the martial music die out, let's hope the words linger to challenge to soldier-service.

God's soldiers are qualified by His standards. Gospel hymns, sung too solemn nowadays, remind us of some of those spiritual qualifications.

> Who is on the Lord's side?
> Who will serve the King?
> Who will be His helpers,
> Other lives to bring?
> Who will leave the world's side?
> Who will face the foe?
> Who is on the Lord's side?
> Who for Him will go?"[3]

## Loyalty

When the confrontation came to Esther, queen of Persia, after spending at least 10 years living in security, in luxury, in a position of prestige, she risked it all for loyalty to God and His people. With a death sentence hanging over the heads of the Jews and realizing that she was the only one exquisitely qualified to refute the works of the Satan-figure Haman, Esther picked up the gauntlet and *fought.* How easily she could have shut out the cries of those who were unable to fight for themselves—outside the walls of the palace—and retreated to her own quarters. No one would have been the wiser.

"Your majesty, . . . *I and my people* have been sold for destruction and slaughter and annihilation. . . . The adversary and enemy is this vile Haman" (Esther 7:3,4,6, italics added).

Let us declare ourselves to be *for* all that God is *for,* and *against* all that God is *against!* We must be willing to face the enemy of our souls, our families, our churches, and identify him. Then, at the risk of our personal comfort (ouch) and security (ouch) declare our identification with the Captain of our salvation, and stand against sin.

> Stand up, stand up for Jesus,
> Stand in His strength alone;
> The arm of flesh will fail you,
> Ye dare not trust your own;
> Put on the gospel armor,
> Each piece put on with prayer,
> Where duty calls or danger,
> Be never wanting there.[4]

### Preparedness

Have you ever heard of a "spiritual streaker"? One who wears the helmet of salvation and one of the other pieces of necessary armor! Downright foolish is the Christian who attempts to stand for Christ without being prepared, fully equipped; without the benefit of the protection and power of the Ephesians 6 list of God's provision:

*The belt of truth* (Eph. 6:14); the belt or girdle covering the body in strength and support. Truth of the Word of God in our minds, in our hearts (see Josh. 1:8) will deal with our problem of confusion.

*The breastplate of righteousness* (6:14); the covering

for our hearts—from which flow all the issues of life—is to be His righteousness. Claiming His forgiveness for our self-righteousness, this part of our preparedness deals with our problem of guilt.

*Shoes of peace and witness* (see 6:15). As a child we sang, "Be careful little feet where you go, there's a father up above, and He's looking down in love, oh, be careful little feet where you go!" These shoes signify a daily desire to walk in His paths, and a preparation to share Jesus Christ. Can these shoes deal with our problem of purposelessness?

*The shield of faith* (6:16); "Without faith it is impossible to please God" (Heb. 11:6). Can you picture warriors of long ago going into battle with their large shields (often larger than the soldier himself)? As the enemy approached, the shields were lined up in front of the soldiers making a wall of protection against that first awful onslaught of arrows. Perhaps we need to shine our shields and line up with the other soldiers as a first line of defense against temptation. This shield of faith can deal with our problem of temptation.

*The helmet of salvation* (Eph. 6:17). Let our thoughts be brought into His captivity and our minds be assured that what Jesus Christ won for you and me at Calvary— our salvation—is our possession! Let this assurance deal with our problem of doubt.

*The sword of the Spirit, which is the word of God* (6:17). This is our weapon, the only part of the armor that is for offense. The application of the Word of God to the conscience will deal with our problem of attitude. Following Jesus' example (see Matt. 4) we can fight off Satan by the proper application of Scripture itself.

*Prayer—the ultimate weapon* (see 6:18). The *Amplified Bible* helps us with these words: "Pray at all times— on every occasion, in every season—in the Spirit, with all [manner of] prayer and entreaty. To that end keep alert and watch with strong purpose *and* perseverance, interceding in behalf of all the saints (God's consecrated people)." Is our lack of victory related directly to our carelessness in prayer? Let this weapon deal with our problem of powerlessness!

## Obedience

Truehearted, wholehearted, faithful and loyal,
King of our lives, by Thy grace we will be;
Under the standard exalted and royal,
Strong in Thy strength we will battle
for Thee.
Truehearted, wholehearted, fullest allegiance
Yielding henceforth to our glorious King;
Valiant endeavor and loving obedience
Freely and joyously now we would bring.[5]

Obedience is one thing—but *loving, free* and *joyous* obedience is something else! "Truehearted, wholehearted, faithful and loyal," we sing. It is easier to sing it than to do it, don't you think? Remember how the Israelites greeted Moses' news that God had given him some laws for them to obey? "If God says we have to obey them, then we certainly will!" (see Exod. 19:8).

Submission to authority is basic to Christian soldiering. The Israelites found out that they were not all that successful in their "wholehearted obedience."

Submission to anything or anyone is definitely out of style in our situation-ethics, permissive society. But submission to one another, and submission to the laws and principles of our God is the standard of Scripture.

Barbara is an enthusiastic pastor's wife-retreat leader in Texas. In less than 10 years, the retreat ministry from their Baptist church has grown to attract over 1,000 women in two sessions. When someone inquired about her format Barbara was definite and simple in her answer: Several seminars are offered in addition to the general sessions. All retreat first-timers have their seminars scheduled. There are three topics each considers: (1) Spirit-controlled living, (2) the act of marriage, (3)submission to authority.

Soldier-servant-leaders, we not only need to be reminded and often retrained to submit to authority in our lives, but we need to know how to teach this scriptural attitude to our children.

The little boy was standing up in the front seat of the car while his mom drove through the shopping center. "Sit down, Bobby!" Mother instructed as she glanced to the right for traffic.

"I said, sit down! Or I will have to sit you down!"

Reluctantly, Bobby submitted to the tug of his mom on his size four jeans, and sat down. As she started the car after the pause at the stop sign, she heard a small defiant voice mutter, "I'm standing up inside!"

Lots of times in my service to the Lord, I have felt like I was obeying but standing up inside. Then I learned to depend on Philippians 2:12 and 13 and I think it has become the most important part of my soldiering equipment. Let me quote it for you from the *Amplified Bible*: "Therefore, my dear ones, as you have always obeyed [my suggestions], so now, not only [with the enthusiasm you would show] in my presence but much more because I am absent, . . . work out . . . your own salvation . . . [Not in your own strength] for it is God Who is all the while effectually at work in you—energizing and creating in you the power and desire—both to will and to work for His good pleasure and satisfaction and delight."

Looking at my calendar I nearly fainted! Another one of those meetings at which I was scheduled to speak. Tonight of all nights! I was exhausted and couldn't understand how I had missed that note on the calendar until now. I realized that it was a small church, a 25-mile distance from home, and I would probably be speaking without honorarium.

As I prepared supper for my family it was a struggle to get my mind and heart prepared for the evening's responsibility. En route, I prayed aloud—as I often do when alone in the sanctuary of my Chevette—and a small miracle occurred. The Lord gave me the *want to*—the will and the desire to obey Him! As I ponder it now it is not all that small a miracle. Claim it as a part of your equipment.

God has promised to give you the desire to obey; presume upon that promise so that you can obey with gladness.

It was a grand evening at that little church and the Lord blessed us all, especially me, with the exhilaration of being in the right place at the right time—obediently.

I left humbly, clutching the gift of three cakes of perfumed soap as my honorarium. It may not have put gas in our tank, but the Lord gave the victory in another skirmish with myself!

### Confrontation

"This day I defy the ranks of Israel! Give me a man and let us fight each other" (1 Sam. 17:10). The challenge rang out across the battleground in Judah. Goliath was at it again, and the terrified brothers of a certain young shepherd boy were among the quivering army of Israel. David, the little brother, came tripping and running to deliver the CARE package from home. David inquired as to what the commotion was all about, and then rather naively asked the brave soldiers why someone hadn't taken Goliath at his challenge.

David found his way to King Saul and volunteered for the fight. Without wasting a minute, Saul responded to David by handing him his own armor. It was not exactly a one-size-fits-all outfit, and little David rattled around in the king's defense mechanism!

Have you thought about confronting any Goliaths lately?

How has God been preparing you for soldiering?

There are giant obstacles to service out there—like limited time for ministries you would love to be involved in, or young children at home who need you so much, or negative attitudes of "other soldiers," even lack of proper equipment. How many other obstacles to service and witness can you add to the list?

All you bring to the battle is a loyalty to Christ and His cause and the preparation of child rearing, perhaps Sunday School teaching, regular attendance at the women's organization, some skills retained from long-ago jobs. They don't seem to "fit" as you confront the larger and more awesome challenge of doing battle against the sinful pressures on the family, the humanistic influences in education, the apathy that debilitates in some churches. Let's do what little David did!

He laid down the unfamiliar armor and dressed himself in that to which he was most accustomed (for you it could be the familiar armor of the godly woman which you have worn for years!) and yelled out to the waiting crowd and to his adversary, "You come against me with sword and spear and javelin, but I come against you in the name of the Lord Almighty, the God of the armies of Israel, whom you have defied. . . . All those gathered here will know that it is not by sword or spear that the Lord saves; for the battle is the Lord's, and he will give all of you into our hands" (1 Sam. 17:45,47).

*Loyalty—Preparedness—Obedience*—just some of the qualifications for soldiering. We could quickly add to the list: fitness, discipline, a spirit of sacrifice, alertness, courage, and on and on. With a list like this there would be little hope of recruiting anyone for action who has a low self-esteem!

"Take [with me] your share of the hardships *and* suffering [which you are called to endure] as a good (first class) soldier of Christ Jesus. No soldier when in service gets entangled in the enterprises of [civilian] life; his aim is to satisfy and please the one who enlisted him" (2 Tim. 2:3,4, *AMP*).

Most of us know little about real suffering; many of us serve in affluent churches. Nor do we pursue suffering on any battlefront. Your share of suffering will undoubtedly look different from mine. Is part of it, however, that struggle over self and selfishness and desire for comfortable, convenient ministries? Words like *obedience, loyalty, courage* are hard ones, and the glorious truth of this word from the Word of God is that the One who enlisted you will provide you with all that you need to please Him. He will give courage, power, equipment, and even the victory.

### Recruiting Others

With a dependence on the Commander, let's consider some principles for recruiting others. It is the most difficult part of leadership—helping others to become involved, challenging to service. Recruitment of others involves risk; *your* reputation is at stake. To enlist another is tantamount to endorsement of a project or ministry. An effective recruiter is one who has already enlisted herself, wears the uniform of identification, has submitted to the disciplines of the project, and is ready for anything.

The Bible is packed with battle accounts that give us some of God's principles for recruiting His armies: let's look at Judges 6 and 7, the Gideon story.

The angel of the Lord came to Gideon and announced to him that the Lord was with him and had a challenging new assignment for him. After hedging—and going through some special object lessons for confirmation—Gideon found that he was *still* God's chosen leader! And what a battle lay ahead. The Midianites had literally reduced God's people to a frightened destitute group of penitent people. God had allowed them to be conquered because of their following after other gods.

But now, mercifully, the time had come for God to lead the Israelites into a much-needed victory. Outnumbering the Israelites, and confident of winning once again, the Midianites were lolling about in leisure.

Gideon sent out a call for volunteers as God had ordered—32,000 responded!

"The army is too big!"

"Too big? Lord, have you seen the Midianite army encamped down there? We need every warm body we can get!"

"Gideon, send home all those who are timid and frightened."

Here is principle #1: *Invest your energies in the most effective place.* Too much energy is expended trying to convince those who do not have  a heart for the battle; you need the energy and spiritual strength for the battle itself.

We must come to the point in our ministry where we say, "God, help me to know the area in which you want me to fight." For example, God might want you to try to enlist the majority of God's people out there. But when there's a battle all kinds of excuses are offered. "I have this situation at home"; "My priorities, you know"; "I'm really awfully busy already." And on and on and on. Perhaps you can help allay the fears and hesitations of the many who *could* serve—but the battle looms near. So, some of you who realize that the enemy is upon us are needed to make the smaller, already submitted group more effective.

For illustration: Suppose you are the women's leader in your church. It is not too difficult to call a speaker of note, get a meeting on the church calendar and into the bulletin, and even arrange for some decorations and refreshments. Then you have some fliers printed and recruit some music. It is not difficult to enlist many to hear a speaker—particularly one with a dramatic "war story." But it is something else again, as many of you have already discovered, to recruit a committee to commit themselves to visiting a nursing home, or organize the youth retreat and sponsor the event, or create the most dynamite missions conference and follow through.

Let's restate principle #1: Be certain your energies are invested in the most effective place possible, even if it means that you have to gulp and send all the fainthearted home!

"Now, Gideon, send more of them home!"

"LORD!"

"Take them to the spring. Divide them into two groups decided by the way they drink. In Group 1 will be all the men who cup the water in their hands to get it to their mouths and lap it like dogs. In Group 2 will be those who kneel, with their mouths in the stream (see Judg. 7:5).

Only 300 of the men drank from their hands; all the others drank with their mouths in the stream.

Could this be principle #2? *Release those who lie down and lap.* Let those go who are more intent on their personal needs and satisfaction than they are on the defeat of the enemy just over the hill. Keep that small group—for Gideon, just 300—who realize that they do have needs but they are still on the alert, with their provided weapons poised. We will work with that smaller group, that company of the committed.

"Lord, there are so many of them, and so few of us!"

"Gideon, they only have weapons and battle strategy. I am going to give you the victory with a strategy that will confound them. You are going to fight this battle on my terms. You will fight with the strangest of all possible weapons—torches and pitchers. In the middle of the night, with the army divided into three groups on the hills surrounding the enemy camp, you will shout, the pitchers will be smashed and the night sky will be ablaze with fire."

"How will this get us the victory, Lord?"

"You won't even have to fight!"

The enemy was indeed confounded, killing each other. There was no opportunity for Gideon to get any glory; the battle had been the Lord's from start to finish!

Principle #3: *Settle it—the closer you get to the battle front, the smaller the army.* Instead of that being a cause for trepidation, let it become a confirmation that the Lord will fight for you. You will not be able to take any credit or glory for being such an outstanding leader who is able to attract great numbers on your ability or personality. Work with that group, regardless of number, people who are qualified by reason of commitment and courage to enter the fray (which can include everything from scrubbing the church kitchen, to helping to rid the community of pornography, to visiting the unlovely in the ghettos of your city) and let the Lord fight for you!

Who will get the credit when a small group of you say, "Lord, we are ready to take the risk of serving you in leadership. It doesn't look like we are going to do very well, but—"

God will say, "Watch! I am setting you up so that you will realize it is 'not by might, nor by power, but by my Spirit' (Zech. 4:6) that you will get the victory. And if you are willing to fight with the weapons of warfare that are not carnal, *but mighty through God* to the pulling down of strongholds, and you are willing to go in my power and give me all the glory, you can claim the victory."

He says, "Take all those with questions in their minds and send them home for now. Take all those who are more concerned with their personal needs than about the fact that the enemy is at hand and send them home for now. Another battle will be faced, and perhaps I will cause some of them to sense the urgency of the training, the urgency of the equipping for ministry, but for now, I choose you, and I am going to get all the glory."

How do I want to be introduced? As a good soldier of Jesus Christ. And I have a heritage of soldiering. Both my

parents and my parents-in-law—as well as David and I—
were officers of the Salvation Army. My grandmother was
born in the same year as the Salvation Army was born in
London's west end. William Booth moved from the
doors of the church and said, "We must reach those who
are still unreached."

The Salvation Army has been a part of my life, for all
of my life, and those *S*'s that are worn on the lapels of the
uniform of Salvationists are significant, not simply to
identify the organization, but as a symbol of the Saved to
Serve slogan of the army's ministry. The discipline of the
flag and the battle as recorded in the several colorful history books written on the Army, is exemplified for me in
the life of the founder's wife, Catherine Booth. I have
read and reread her biography, and she was a good soldier of Jesus Christ.

Let me share with you these words from her story:

"Let us stand together by her open grave in the
autumn twilight. Her twenty-six years of fight and toil in
The Salvation Army are over now, her spirit has been
summoned Home. Listen. The Army Founder himself is
the speaker. He is recalling the forty years which he and
our dear Army Mother had trod together, and his words
sum up better than any other words could do what she
was to our Leader:

" 'If you had had a tree' he said, speaking to the vast
crowd that stood round the grave, 'that had grown up in
your garden, under your window, which for forty years
had been your shadow from the burning sun, whose
flowers had been the adornment and beauty of your life,
whose fruit had been almost the stay of your existence,
and the gardener had come along and swung his glitter-
ing axe and cut it down before your eyes, I think you
would feel as though you had a blank—it might not be a
big one—but a little blank in your life.

" 'If you had had a servant who for all this long time
had served you without fee or reward, who had adminis-

tered, for very love, to your health and comfort, and who suddenly passed away, you would miss that servant.

" 'If you had had a counsellor who, in hours—continually occurring—of perplexity and amazement, had ever advised you, and seldom advised wrong; whose advice you had followed, and seldom had reason to regret it; and the counsellor, while you were in the same intricate mazes of your existence, had passed away, you would miss that counsellor.

" 'If you had had a friend who had understood your very nature, the rise and fall of your feelings, the bent of your thoughts, and the purpose of your existence; a friend whose communion had ever been pleasant—the most pleasant of all other friends—to whom you had ever turned with satisfaction, and your friend had been taken away, you would feel some sorrow at the loss.

" 'If you had had a mother for your children who had cradled and nursed and trained them for the service of the living God, in which you most delighted—a mother, indeed, who had never ceased to bear their sorrows on her heart, and who had been ever willing to pour forth that heart's blood in order to nourish them, and that darling mother had been taken from your side, you would feel it a sorrow.

" 'If you had had a wife, a sweet love of a wife, who for forty years had never given you real cause for grief; a wife who had stood with you, side by side, in the battle's front, who had been a comrade to you, ever willing to interpose herself between you and the enemy, and ever the strongest when the battle was fiercest, and your beloved one had fallen before your eyes, I am sure there would be some excuse for your sorrow.

" 'Well, my comrades, you can roll all these qualities into one personality, and what would be lost in all I have lost in one. There has been taken away from me the light of my eyes, the inspiration of my soul, and we are about to lay all that remains of her in the grave. I have been looking right at the bottom of it here, calculating how soon they may bring and lay me alongside of her, and my cry to God has been that every remaining hour of my life may make me readier to come and join her in death, to go and embrace her in life in the Eternal City.' "[6]

## Notes

1. Adapted from Simeon Stylites.
2. Sabine Baring-Gould, "Onward, Christian Soldiers."
3. Frances R. Havergal, "Who Is on the Lord's Side?"
4. George Duffield, Jr., "Stand Up, Stand Up for Jesus."
5. Frances R. Havergal, "Truehearted, Whole-Hearted."
6. Mildred Duff, *Catherine Booth* (London: Salvationist's Publishing and Supplies, n.d.), pp. 43-45.

# Five

# The Athlete

"If anyone competes as an athlete, he does not receive the victor's crown unless he competes according to the rules" (2 Tim. 2:5).

"The time is now to sign up for this afternoon's tennis round robin," the voice of the program director boomed across the dining room. My husband and I were attending a summer conference and were eager to cooperate with the proposed schedule. David and I really don't have tennis built into our lives, but we signed up! Whatever made me do it I will never know. I put on my J.C. Penney culottes and navy blue sneakers, and David was in his Montgomery Ward work pants, and we proceeded up the hill. I clutched my racquet tightly because the tape was unraveling from the handle (can you expect authentic catgut and suede tape from a discount house?).

Our names were called and we gallantly skipped onto our assigned court. Now I could really see the other participants, and I was psychologically defeated! The women wore tiny, white pleated skirts, pompoms on their pure white tennis shoes (theirs were definitely *not* sneakers!), their hair was coiffed beneath cute white visors that matched their husbands'! I was just trying to be a good sport, and could not have been more relieved when the chief robin (is that what they call the scorekeeper?) indicated that we had lost!

When the bulk of the crowd wound their way back down the hill, David and I met at the net. "How about you and I just playing around and try to hit the ball *to* each other. Let's see how many times we can get it over the net without stopping!"

We worked up to nine times and were hot but elated at the progress. There was one big drawback, however. Can you figure out what it was? The game soon lost its fascination because I would not have known if I had won—because I didn't know the rules!

I can get onto the court, bat the ball back and forth, and look like I am playing the game—there might even be a few watching who are convinced that I am winning, but unless I apply myself to learning and obeying the rules I will never win.

The Scripture teaches me that there are rules for God's athlete, and if we are to be qualified for the prize we must subject ourselves to the training and day-by-day discipline necessary for the game.

Do you know what my husband gave me for Christmas? A tennis dress! It was the most ridiculous looking thing and one size too small, but how I loved him for dreaming big dreams and setting high goals! I had to return it to the exclusive little tennis shop in which he bought it. Did I tell you that I also had to return the matching panties? Now, could I wear lace-trimmed briefs that had embroidered across them TENNIS MOM?

The salespeople were not interested in my story, or why the dress didn't fit but was appreciated anyhow, or much else to do with me. But when the young woman suggested that I exchange the panties for another pair in my size with the words WANNA CHEAT? across them, it was the last straw!

Now I have a nice conservative navy, cotton-knit tennis dress. Should I ever have the courage to appear on a
tennis court again, I have something to wear.

### A Will to Win

A size five friend offered to include me in a group tennis lesson she was coaching. It was there I learned that
some tennis balls are alive and some are dead. It was also
there that I learned a few of the rules, not enough to play
with confidence, but a start. And I learned that I can benefit from more coaching.

The servant-athlete is characterized by a will to win.
There is a philosophy in our society that competition is a
no-no. If there is a winner then there will be a loser.
Nobody likes to be a loser, or be labeled a loser. However, who or what does the Scripture tell us is to be our
adversary? Our opponent? Against what are we to compete? Over what are we to gain mastery?

*Ourselves!* We are not to compete against other
Christians for power or prizes; we are to measure our
progress against ourselves. But we are taught that satisfaction with "how far we have come" or "how well we
are doing" is unsatisfactory—we are to continually press
on, look forward, be transformed.

"Now every athlete who goes into training conducts
himself temperately and restricts himself in all things. . . .
But [like a boxer] I buffet my body—handle it roughly,
discipline it by hardships—and subdue it, for fear that
after proclaiming to others the Gospel and things pertain-
ing to it, I myself should become unfit—not stand the test
and be unapproved" (1 Cor. 9:25, 27, *AMP.*) Competing
against what we are now, we are to grow up into Christ.
And there are rules. It is good exercise to list some of the
RULES given to us as they are given in Ephesians 4 and
5.

● Strip yourself of your former nature—4:22.
● Be constantly renewed in the spirit of your mind—

having a fresh mental and spiritual attitude—4:23,24.

- When angry, do not sin—4:26.
- Leave no room or foothold for the devil—4:27.
- Let the thief steal no more, but rather let him be industrious—4:28.
- Let no foul or polluting language ever come out of your mouth—4:29.
- Do not grieve the Holy Spirit of God—4:30.
- Let all bitterness and wrath and resentment and quarreling be banished from you—4:31.
- And become useful and helpful and kind to one another—4:32.
- Be imitators of God—5:1.
- Immorality and impurity or greediness must not even be named among you—5:3.

Most of us have so much already revealed of God's rules and will for our lives that we don't have time to inquire for more clarification! Let us be athletes who strive for masteries over ourselves, according to the rules.

*Forces of evil!* We must be in condition to struggle and compete not against other people, for "our struggle is not against flesh and blood, but against the rulers, against the authorities, against the powers of this dark world and against the spiritual forces of evil in the heavenly realms" (Eph. 6:12).

Competition is scriptural—but let us be careful about the principles and rules of the Word regarding our opponent.

Judging from progress to this date, I will probably never become a tennis pro, a coach, or even a very good player. Actually, as Ziggy has said, I don't really understand how so many people can get excited about a game where LOVE means NOTHING!

And most of us will never become full-time counselors, but in the context of the servant-athlete let us consider some rules for becoming people-helpers—or coaches.

## A Coach's Characteristics

*A coach, or an athletic people-helper must keep a confidence.*

"A gossip betrays a confidence, but a trustworthy man keeps a secret" (Prov. 11:13). You have heard that there are three means of communication—telephone, telegraph and tell-a-woman! We have not had a good image; we have been labeled as unable to keep a secret or a confidence. The old gossip game has been a topic for fun all too often.

Bursting to tell a juicy morsel! Have we even been known to use a prayer meeting as a spiritual cloak for this weakness in our character? "Tonight I would appreciate prayer for Barbara. It is not necessary for me to share all the details. Just remember to pray for their family, and that the Lord will help before they need to go for professional help. Pray that circumstances will be reversed and a love and communication begin in their home."

What goes on in your mind? Any additions to that "prayer request" are up to the hearers' imagination—and most of us are good at that. May the Lord forgive us for making our prayers news bulletins!

If you will be used of God to help others, you must be able to keep a confidence. "Help me, Lord, to keep my mouth shut and my lips sealed" (Ps. 141:3, *TLB*).

*A coach has to have compassion.* "If anyone has this world's good—resources for sustaining life—and sees his brother and fellow believer in need, yet closes his heart of compassion against him, how can the love of God live and remain in him?" (1 John 3:17, *AMP*).

The dictionary says that compassion is sympathy and tenderheartedness. A compassionate coach must learn to listen to understand, not to criticize. What does the helpee want? Permanent help or temporary relief? Listen with a tender heart.

An old general of the Salvation Army wrote from his heart, this chorus to one of the many hymns:

Except I am moved with compassion
How dwellest Thy Spirit in me?
In word and in deed
Burning love is my need
I know I can find this in Thee.[1]


*A coach will be conscientious* about principle over preference or pressure.

"You have laid down precepts that are to be fully obeyed" (Ps. 119:4). In an article in *Moody Monthly* entitled "Let's Let Women Counsel Women," Naomi Taylor Wright said:

"Pastors should create the opportunity for godly older women in their congregations to teach and counsel younger women.

"Such a woman must really know God's Word, not be judgmental, and be able to speak the truth in love. She may be a woman whose family has grown and gone or she may be a young woman who is spiritually mature—'older' in Christ.

"She must be one who loves her husband and home, is compassionate toward others, is accustomed to bearing spiritual fruit. She must be teachable herself.

"She must know how to introduce people to Christ and how to use God's Word in counseling. She must believe in the permanency of marriage. She must believe that scriptural principles work. . . . She must believe that God is 'the God of hope.' "[2]

You will be on very dangerous ground—the sinking sand kind—if you allow your personal preferences to enter the helping situation. It is the principles that stand the test. A principle expresses a changeless truth that can serve as a guide for conduct or procedure. Principles are fundamental laws of eternal truth.

Rev. James Braga says that principles have several features: (1) Each is a positive, not a negative, statement;

(2) each is a clear or incisive declaration; (3) each is a truth which is always valid; (4) each is an established law, basic for life or conduct. If these are true, could it be that there are conflicting principles in the Word? No!

" 'Eye for eye, and tooth for tooth.' Go ahead and get back at her!" Is that what Jesus said in Matthew 5:38? Yes, but the principle is in the next verse: "But I tell you, Do not resist an evil person. If someone strikes you on the right cheek, turn to him the other also. . . . Love your enemies and pray for those who persecute you" (vv. 39,44).

See if you can decide whether these are principles or preferences:

a. Women must not work outside their homes.

b. Haircuts should reveal the entire ear.

c. The man is the head of the home.

d. Children are to live in obedience to their parents in the Lord.

e. Women should not wear pants to church.

These are simplistic examples. Hopefully, you have been able to identify the principles! An athlete-coach must be conscientious to use the Word of God carefully and correctly, basing counsel on principles.

*A coach will have courage to confront.*

"Don't think of him as an enemy, but speak to him as you would to a brother who needs to be warned" (2 Thess. 3:15, *TLB*). Paul, in this letter, is counseling regarding believers who are lazy. After the exhortation to get to work, he gives that direction on how to help and exhort others. This characteristic requires courage, but perhaps requires more wisdom than anything else!

Confrontation is sometimes made in anger: "It is about time someone let you have it! And I have decided that I will be that person!"

It takes courage and wisdom, with a non-judgmental attitude, to help the helpee identify the root problem. It takes courage and self-control to guide the helpee to make right choices, if warning and confrontation is the Lord's leading for the helper.

*Care to realize personal limitations.* "If you want to know what God wants you to do, ask him, and he will gladly tell you, for he is always ready to give a bountiful supply of wisdom to all who ask him; he will not resent it" (Jas. 1:5, *TLB*).

There is a certain ego-building element in being asked for help or counsel. And there is a tendency to respond to questions with a kind of heady authority as if we are the fount of all wisdom. Occasionally, at least occasionally, a credible counselor/helper will have to admit that the situation is baffling and needs to be referred to someone *more qualified* to help—perish the thought!

A good friend, who is also a fine speaker, decided it was time to have a brochure printed. This would simplify responses to invitations as to what she *did*? She began to list various areas of interest and areas in which she felt qualified to speak (she is also a gifted counselor), and was completely chagrined! Not even the Bionic Woman could be an expert in all of those assorted fields! Realizing that her effectiveness would be impaired by trying to speak to too many areas, she wisely and prayerfully limited her expertise.

Often our helping can be simply guiding a helpee through a concordance—either before, with, or after a counseling session. Do not hesitate to reveal your inadequacy and affirm the adequacy of Jesus Christ.

Practically speaking, it is a good idea to become acquainted with resources in your church and community for problem solving. As you assume leadership in your service, make a list or resource file to which you can refer as the need arises. Check these resources for yourself, making certain that you can endorse the principles on which the help is built.

Be able to clarify and simplify. "Since we have such a huge crowd of men of faith watching us from the grandstands, let us strip off anything that slows us down or holds us back, and especially those sins that wrap themselves so tightly around our feet and trip us up" (Heb. 12:1, *TLB*). Listen attentively, then be the coach who will help to clear rather than confuse with complicating counsel. Here are some steps to living more simply:

1. Simply believe that God loves you, and that love is more than a *nothing* in tennis. Simple, profound, steadying. Henrietta Mears, founder of Gospel Light Publications, was asked late in her life if she had the opportunity to begin again what would she change. Her answer was *simple*: "I would just believe God!"

"We know how much God loves us because we have felt his love and because we believe him when he tells us that he loves us dearly" (1 John 4:6, *TLB*).

2. Live one day at a time. "So don't be anxious about tomorrow. God will take care of your tomorrow too. Live one day at a time." (Matt. 6:34, *TLB*, italics added).

3. Let go of all that is wrong. "So get rid of all that is wrong in your life, both inside and outside" (Jas 1:21, *TLB*).

4. Learn to visualize solutions. God says you have won! "It is he who makes us victorious through Jesus Christ our Lord! So, my dear brothers, since future victory is sure, be strong and steady, always abounding in the Lord's work, for you know that nothing you do for the Lord is ever wasted" (1 Cor. 15:57,58, *TLB*).

5. Keep your eye on the ball—there is a goal. We are surrounded by a lot of encouragers in those Hebrews 12 grandstands. Don't look too much to OTHERS.

*A coach challenges action.* "So ever since we first heard about you we have kept on praying and asking God to help you understand what he wants you to do; asking him to make you wise about spiritual things; and asking that the way you live will always please the Lord and honor him, so that you will always be doing good, kind things for others, while all the time you are learning to know God better and better" (Col. 1:9,10, *TLB*).

Be a coach who has some helpful ideas to aid the helpee to take a step toward being part of the solution herself. (a) attend church regularly; (b) read at least a small portion of the Bible daily; (c) read helpful, encouraging books (you suggest a list); (d) borrow good cassette tapes; (e) pray with thanksgiving—it is therapeutic! (Griping to God in the name of prayer is self-demoralizing.); (f) do *one* thing each day to be part of the answer (wash the kitchen floor, make a phone call, clean the garage, buy yourself an ice cream cone, or even as Ziggy recommends "try not to faint"!); (g) memorize an "old man's favorite Scripture verse": "It came to pass" and "Expect God to act (Ps. 42:11, *TLB*).

*Be a cheerful coach.* Is it principle or preference or just personality that makes us cheerful? "A cheerful heart is good medicine" (Prov. 17:22). Be a cheerful coach! When a certain mother-Sunday School teacher enrolled in a local college for a theology course that would help her with her teaching, her 10-year-old son Mark inquired, "Mom, are you going out for cheerleader?" Ladies, let's all go out for cheerleader! In this era of self-styled psychologists, and trainers and trainees in self-therapy, let you and me be the front-runners of a Christ-styled philosophy that says in Jesus' own words: "Here on earth you will have many trials and sorrows; but cheer up, for I have overcome the world" (John 16:33, *TLB*).

"Now, not all godly older women who know their Bibles inside and out are gifted to counsel. But those who are can work with women one-to-one." Picking up on the "Let's Let Women Counsel Women" article, the writer continues, "They will recognize when a counselee may be part of her own problem. They can say things in love a man could never get away with. They will not be protective or transfer sexual affection to their counselee, although there may be a deep mutual appreciation.

"A woman counselee will be less apt to accuse her female counselor of being incapable of understanding her problems. She obviously can't accuse her of 'male chauvinism.' This will rob her of many reasons for rejecting painful but corrective suggestions."[3]

Mrs. Wright describes their Cris-Town Bible Study in Phoenix which offers a class for women who want to learn how to counsel other women with marriage problems: "We seek to reinforce God's teachings on the home by teaching principles of counseling, what to listen for as they counsel, Scriptures to use, and homework to give. We discuss case studies in small groups. Then we occasionally have the women whose study has just been discussed come and give her testimony. Our trainees then compare how they analyzed the root problem and what sort of counsel worked. We emphasize memorizing Scripture. Our case study analysis sheet is divided into five columns. Each trainee writes a heading for each column: the counselee's problem, her solution, her results, God's solution (with verses), and ultimate results."[4]

Little Janie came into the house and told her mother that her friend Susie had dropped her doll and it had broken.

"Did you help her fix it?" Janie's mother asked.

"No, we couldn't fix it," Janie replied, "but I helped her cry!" Yes, most of us will probably never hang out a counselor's shingle, but let's at least help one another cry!

## Goal to Go!

Bev is a young mom in excellent physical condition, and probably wears a size five (which I personally think should be against the law!). Three or four years ago she decided she needed some exercise and she bounded out of her South Minneapolis front door just as friend-husband came in for supper. Exhilarated with positive action on her afternoon decision, Bev waved and was off. She ran two blocks and collapsed on the sidewalk. "Stay with it!" said a strange voice from inside. And she did—working up to a few blocks and even a mile as the days went by.

Now, around a lake! See all the neighbors looking at the funny lady running while her kids cheer her on . . . see Bev run! The snow falls, and Bev keeps running; springtime arrives, and Bev runs on.

The announcement of the Boston Marathon was a tantalizing goal—but could she make it? There were qualifications to meet, and daily, grueling longer distances to be gained.

She went to Boston in April and gleefully, determinedly looked forward to achieving her goal. What had been a long-term goal now appeared on her near horizon. She had followed the rules, and now came the test. She bore a MINNESOTA banner across her chest and a number on her back for identification; the Gatorade was being cooled.

Excitement mounted and then peaked as the starting gun was fired. Thousands ran along the people-lined streets. Bev waved and smiled at the encouragers—at least for the first several miles. It is said that the 26 miles of the marathon race is beyond the limit of human endurance, but Bev finished—perhaps after twilight, I don't know, but she ran the race and achieved her goal!

Did she win? That's a matter of viewpoint, don't you think? If you mean, did she come in first? Then of course the answer is no; but if you mean, did she finish the course? Then comes a resounding YES!

At times during those last miles the thought crept in, "Why am I doing this? Nobody said I had to go through this! I just want to die!" She won the prize of knowing that she had reached far down inside and begun to feel what it is like to live beyond your own capacity.

She ran again the next year—and the next. Running

daily has become part of her own discipline and regimen. Each marathon she runs has the goal of bettering her previous time. She wants to do better, reach harder, compete against herself!

"I am still not all I should be but I am bringing all my energies to bear on this one thing: Forgetting the past and looking forward to what lies ahead, I strain to reach the end of the race and receive the prize for which God is calling us up to heaven because of what Christ Jesus did for us" (Phil. 3:1,14 *TLB*). Now *that's* a prize! A real goal to be won. "Yes, everything else is worthless when compared with the priceless gain of knowing Christ Jesus my Lord" (Phil. 3:8, *TLB*).

To be God's athlete-servant-leader we must have the goal clear. Why did Bev keep on running? No one was whipping her. Was the world any different because one young mother was "pressing toward a mark"? Why should she not just give up? She hadn't a breath of a chance of winning the race.

At the nineteenth mile Bev came to the end of herself. Is that part of the achievement of God's highest goals in our lives? Come to the end of yourself? Acknowledge that you will not be able to finish in your own strength? It is at that moment that God is able to release His power to do for you what you cannot do for yourself.

More often than not we drop out because of our inadequacy in personal relationships, in personal discipline, and in our leadership roles. "We are not able." God says, I knew it all along! Begin to appropriate my supernatural power and "run and don't be weary; walk and don't faint" (see Isa. 40:31).

My prayer is that the Lord will give me a touch of that supernatural power in my life. I am sick of the insipid existence that does only what I know I can do. I want to reach out, set higher goals, experience what it means to depend upon the resources of my God. I must ask the Lord to help me to establish priorities that, when I consistently follow them, will enable me to reach worthier goals.

"In a race, everyone runs but only one person gets first prize. So run your race to win. To win the contest you must deny yourselves many things that would keep you from doing your best. An athlete goes to all this trouble just to win a blue ribbon or a silver cup, but we do it for a heavenly reward that never disappears. So I run straight to the goal with purpose in every step" (1 Cor. 9:24-26, *TLB*).

Bev had a goal.

Paul had a goal, a mark, a prize for which he was willing to expend all his energies. The priceless gain of knowing Christ.

Perhaps we will just play a game of semantics, but then again as we consider some well-used words you will gain a small prize of a new insight about targets in your life.

Take the word *purpose*, for example. What is the purpose of your life? Right! To glorify God and enjoy Him forever. How do you fulfill that purpose? The Scripture teaches that there are many ways to glorify God: with our praise (see Ps. 50:23); with our witness (see Matt. 5:16); in our suffering (see Rom. 8:17).

Now consider *goals*. Can you think of the difference between a goal and a purpose? Ted Engstrom, in his book *Strategy for Living*, helped me with this statement: The difference between goals and purposes is simply their measurability. Goals are measurable targets. You know when your goal has been reached.[5]

A third word—*priorities*. Priorities are what you do, to realize the goals to fulfill the purpose.

Let's illustrate: My purpose is to glorify God. One of the ways I do this is to keep my body under subjection and in good condition. And would you believe it, I am 20 pounds overweight! I have been playing lost and found with that same 20 pounds for 20 years. Actually, I have lost hundreds of pounds over the years! Erma Bombeck says that she has lost so much weight she should be dangling from a charm bracelet about now!

Well, I set the goal to lose those 20 pounds. As I organize my life or set my priorities, that goal will be achieved. I will have to make that diet and discipline one of my priorities. Up front. First—at least for a time.

Tell me that you have experienced the thrill of reaching a goal weight! I will not inquire as to how long you stayed there, but life is full of small victories (and occasional defeats!).

I cannot measure the purpose but I certainly know when I have reached a goal. It is when our priorities are not in line that our goals are elusive and we are frustrated about our purpose.

The general lineup for setting our priorities might be:
1.  Our commitment to God
2.  Our commitment to our family
3.  Our commitment to the family of God
4.  Our commitment to the work of God.

One of the reasons for frustration in my own very busy life is pigeon-holing the activities of my day. Too much compartmentalizing. Sometimes when I am shopping for groceries my mind is flooded with all the other things I need to do to get ready for a meeting, or typing for my husband, or the fact that I spend such a brief time with the Lord. The Lord brings calm to me by whispering simply: "Daisy, I will help you to be a both-and not an either-or." Because of my life's purpose and my basic commitments, I must wear several hats. Many times the Lord shows me how those priorities or commitments can be worked out simultaneously with joy!

One of my goals is to see my children grow into maturity in Jesus Christ and to be occupied in His service, whatever their occupation. This is not the purpose for which I live, but it is a goal because of my purpose.

Given this goal, my next step is to order the activity of

my life, or my priorities, to make it possible for me to achieve that goal. One of my priorities, then, must be prayer! Another for me might be to help to bring some extra income to our home to support our daughter attending a Christian college.

Possibly my work is for a Christian organization serving our community. Can you see how I am working out my commitment to God, to my family, to His family and to His work, all at the same time?

As an athlete-leader one of the dangers we must face is setting our goals too low. Have you experienced that tendency to discouragement because of mediocrity? Busywork? The goals are too low. Let the goals for your ministry be lofty ones—excellence—to fulfill the purposes of God.

"This year we are going to have five combined meetings." Why? The answer is slow in coming. The goals for those meetings are indefinite. Just *meeting* is not an adequate goal. What do you want to see happen? What will you ask God to do for you and all who will attend?

Programming without goals does not constitute a ministry.

Activity or filling up the calendar is not synonymous with success. We tend to fulfill our goals when some tension is applied. Even a rubber band is good for nothing unless stretched!

You have the highest possible purpose. Set high goals and bring your priorities in line to achieve those goals.

In my book, *Why Doesn't Somebody Do Something?*, I have quoted my husband. When I have been tempted to expend energies in trivia, and run around in circles with things or situations that just don't matter and are not contributing to the goal, David has said, "Daisy, that just is not a high enough hill to die on!"

Bev had her ticket to go to Boston for the race. Ann Kiemel lived in Boston, and Bev had been inspired by reading all of Ann's books and decided to call her: "Hi,

Ann. I'm Bev." They had lunch together the day after the marathon.

In Ann's book, on April 17 these words are recorded:
"lunch today with Bev Wenshau.
she came from Minneapolis with her family to
run the
Boston marathon yesterday.
she'd written ahead, hoping to meet me
. . . had read all my books.
suddenly, over lunch, she said . . .
'ann, you could run a marathon. you're lean
. . . and disciplined,
you could.'
i looked at this young woman . . . just my
age . . . a hero to me.
and at that moment, today, in the parker
house hotel,          -
downtown boston, the dream was really born.
to be a runner . . . to go for broke . . . not
to quit . . .
God helping me.
i wonder what this really means?
i wonder."[6]

Bev and Ann became fast friends. You will see Bev's picture in the book. She paced Ann several months later when Ann took a group of Boston's children to the Holy Land—Bev paced her running around the Sea of Galilee.

It was April, 1980, and Ann was one of several women speakers in Washington, D.C. As she was announced and stepped to the microphone to speak, she seemed unsteady on her feet. "I still have bandages on my feet! But I finished the Boston marathon!"

From the back jacket of *I'm Running to Win*:
"no one can really understand what it costs
or means to be faithful . . .
unless he has tried to do that.

the people on the periphery, cheering the
   winners,
really have no comprehension of what it
   meant
to be out there running those miles.
   they thought it looked great, and they were
impressed with people who could . . .
   but they couldn't know inside what it really
      feels like
to put yourself on the line . . . to compete . . .
      to feel the pressure and the strain and
      the throb in your whole body.
   i think it's the same as being true with
      Jesus.
   unless one has really tried to be faithful . . .
      really paid some price for faithfulness
      . . .

   one doesn't understand the cost or the
      great reward . . . the pain and the great
      joy."[7]

"In a race, everyone runs but only one person gets
first prize. So run your race to win" (1 Cor. 9:24 *TLB*).

## Notes

1. *The Salvation Army Songbook* (New York: Salvation
Army Supplies and Printing, n.d.), p. 478.
2. Naomi Taylor Wright, "Let's Let Women Counsel
Women, *Moody Monthly* , November, 1980, p. 41.
3. Ibid.
4. Ibid.
5. Edward R. Dayton and Ted W. Engstrom, *Strategy for
Living* (Ventura, CA: Regal Books, 1976), p. 49.
6. Ann Kiemel, *I'm Running to Win* (Wheaton, IL: Tyn-
dale House Publishers, 1980), p. 18.
7. Ibid., back jacket.

## Six

# The Farmer

"Work hard, like a farmer who gets paid well if he raises a large crop" (2 Tim. 2:6, *TLB*).

Mrs. Craig was a cottage mother at Lytton Children's Home in Sonoma County, California. Her second calling was definitely that of farmer. Twenty-two, or sometimes even more, little boys were in her charge. They were almost the youngest group in our home of 130 boys and girls, and ranged in age from 9 to 11.

There was no discussion, but a clear assumption, that every one of the boys would be expected to do his stint in the garden. Ma Craig had walked it all out near the cottage, and measured and planned the garden. Then the boys were enlisted. She enticed them with visions of buttered corn on the cob, watermelon feeds, as well as all manner of goodies to be purchased from the sale of their produce. What pride those kids took in their garden! Mulch and manure, sunshine and sweat, planting and prodding, working and weeding, in a never-ending cycle.

One unforgettable night, the boys from Oaks Cottage treated the entire home, staff and kids, to a golden dinner of home-grown corn, with fruit salad for dessert! You know, of course, that Ma Craig was growing a lot more than vegetables—she was growing boys!

Let me tell you about a boy that needed more cultivation than some of her charges. Leroy Henderson, jet black and from Los Angeles County Juvenile Hall.

One day a group of beautiful young people came to lead a Sunday morning Mother's Day service for the children. An invitation was given to receive Christ. This invitation was often extended, but when Leroy heard it this time, it seemed like God was talking to his heart in a special way and he gleefully responded.

He decided that day to follow Jesus and respond to the tiny little bit of light that flooded his heart. A personable young man spent time with Leroy, counseling, sharing and praying with him. But praying and unfamiliar reading of the Bible was not going to come easily to Leroy.

He went to his cottage that evening and got down by his bed and tried to pray. Above his head, flying back and forth in that room in which 13 other boys were housed, flew everything from socks to baseballs. Leroy could stand it no longer and stood up and said, "Listen, you guys, I am trying to pray—so, be quiet!"

Leroy knelt again but this time there was loud talking, hammering and pouncing even on his bed. Leroy lifted his head again and said, "Okay, you guys, I told you once I gotta' pray—so SHUT UP!"

Donning his football helmet for protection, he knelt again. But the kids were not about to give up that easily on their harassment.

Waiting as long as he could, Leroy Henderson jumped to his feet, and yelled out for all the world to hear, at the top of his lungs, "Listen you guys, that guy told me to pray and I am going to pray if I have to kill every single one of you to do it!"

"Determination! Misguided—but determination, that

is for sure!

I will never forget Leroy Henderson. He promised that after he made his first million dollars he would buy David and me our very own church. I wonder where Leroy Henderson is now—

Ma Craig planted so much seed into the lives of her boys. Who would dare to measure the fruit produced in their lives as the years have passed from one season to the other?

"Which is best, Allis-Chalmers or John Deere?"

The boys confronted me with a question I really was not prepared to answer. I had watched their discussion from the camp office window and figured they would soon have to seek out a referee—two kids right off the farm, unable to leave their loyalties behind even for a week at camp. Didn't someone say once, "You can take the boy off the farm, but you can't take the farm out of the boy"? It's true.

"Well, kids, I would like to help you, but I don't speak farm too well," was all I could come up with.

I had been raised on the sidewalks of New York and other big cities, and when a farmer talks to me about walking beans or doing all sorts of things with oats, and the amount of rainfall, and putting everything aside—even school—for harvesttime, well, it baffles me. And it fascinates me.

The Word of God speaks farm.

How much it has to say about our growing up into the fullness of our God. We are pictured as both the garden and the gardener. The farmer and the soil.

In this chapter we will consider the farmer, and how you as a woman of God can exemplify the finest qualities of a farmer as you develop your servant-leadership abilities.

We will talk about cultivating committees and weeding out your resource file, as well as the country parson's idea of a productive garden.

First, we will talk about what we are, then what we can do. Get up and grow—a recurring theme in the Scripture. We are to be like trees planted by the rivers of water that bringeth forth its fruit in its season (see Ps. 1:3). Let's do some digging and find five steps to fruit-bearing maturity. Call it tips on cultivating a Christian!

## There Is a Time for Planting

"The seed is the word of God," it says in Luke 8:11. And in Isaiah we read that the good seed will not return void; it will accomplish all that God has planned (see Isa. 55:10,11).

Most of us have had an abundance of good seed sown in our lives. In this day of mass evangelism, local and small-group Bible studies, the electronic church, neighborhood ministries, Christian books by the millions—there is no excuse for not having enough seed sown in our lives to have produced an abundant harvest by this time!

How can I ever thank the Lord for grandparents on both sides of our family whose first priority it was to sow good seed in our lives. My mother and dad saw to it that their daughters were early confronted with the claims of Christ, and kept right on sowing good seed.

You are undoubtedly reading this book because someone else has already sown good seed in your life. And it has taken root. Think about how that happened in your life the first time. Was it your grandmother taking you to Sunday School where you heard the Word of God, or someone inviting you to a church service where the gospel was being preached, or to a Bible study, or was it a Gideon Bible in a motel room? Thank God for the faithfulness of sowers.

Just offshore, from a boat, Jesus taught about soil and its characteristics. Surely there were farmers listening because Jesus lost no opportunity to communicate through that which was known to His hearers, leading them to the unknown deeper truths.

"A farmer went out to sow his seed." Some seed fell on the hard pathway. The birds came and ate the seed before it even got past the crust and hardened topsoil. Is this ever like your heart? Have we had so much good seed sown that the Word has long since been snatched away through carelessness or familiarity? Can you still hear the voice of God? Or has your heart been crusted over through years and years of church attendance without the Word taking root? It seems that the Pharisees listening to Jesus had already closed their minds to His teaching.

Lloyd Ogilvie in his book, *The Autobiography of God*, declares that customs, traditions and political beliefs can make Pharisees out of church members. When we hear a truth "that we do not live out, we block our sensitivity to hear further truth. . . . The greatest single cause of impaired hearing of fresh truth is the refusal to live what we already know."[1]

"What was sown on rocky places is the man who hears the word and at once receives it with joy. But since he has no root, he lasts only a short time" (Matt. 13:20,21).

Dr. Ogilvie states that bedrock is covered over with a thin layer of soil. The seed is lodged in this soil and takes root. But the roots quickly reach the impenetrable rock. Because the roots are not allowed to grow deeply and are denied the replenishment of depth nourishment, the surface plant withers in the sun. It cannot sustain its initial growth. What does this have to say about our hearing and our hearts?

Remember that the heart is the inner core of intellect, emotion and will. If one aspect of our hearts is penetrated to the exclusion of the rest, our hearing will be faulty. We will know immediate growth, but no lasting maturity. Dr. Ogilvie suggests these three kinds of Christians:[2] (1) the emotional Christian—beginning with great enthusiasm, but easily thrown off balance; (2) the intellectual Christian—has not allowed Christ to deal with emotions and attitudes; (3) the volitional Christian—perhaps intellectually sound and emotionally free but withered if we refuse to do God's will in the painful areas of obedience. Have you known at least one time in your life when you felt like you were shallow soil?

Thorny ground Christians are those whose hearts are crowded out, and the good seed is choked denying the possibility of fruit. "He does less and less for God," *The Living Bible* says (Matt. 13:22). There are just too many voices clamoring for attention.

"When is a heart overcrowded? When is the good seed unable to grow because the resources of thought, energy, creativity and time are depleted on secondary loyalty to the thorns? If there is no time for listening to God in Bible study and prolonged meditation, we are too busy. When we are too distracted by duties and responsibilities to grow as persons, we are over-involved. When we have no time for people and are not reproducing our faith in them, we are dangerously close to missing the reason we were born."[3]

Hurray for the good soil! It is the hearing heart. "But what was sown on good soil is the man who hears the word and understands it. He produces a crop, yielding a hundred, sixty or thirty times what was sown" (Matt. 13:23).

The chief characteristic of the good soil, the productive plot, the victory garden, is its receptivity to the seed. Luke 8:15 tells us that the good soil "stands for those with a noble and good heart, who hear the word, retain it, and by persevering produce a crop."

The difference between these kinds of soil is solely in their receptivity to the seed, and over that we have only our free will to consider! Choose to receive the Word of God, to obey it and to allow God to make it produce!

### There Is a Time for Cultivating

May your roots go down deep into the soil of God's marvelous love" (Eph. 3:17, *TLB*). If the life of Christ has found lodging in your heart, through the reception of the seed of His Word, then you must cooperate with the elements to cultivate that new, struggling shoot. Growth is the only evidence of life it is said, and when we are born into the Kingdom, naturally we begin to grow: in faith and understanding; in love for Christ and others; in influence for Jesus; and in production of fruit.

Try as we will, we cannot make ourselves grow! It is "only God who makes things grow" (1 Cor. 3:7). But we can and must respond to the elements of His love and care—showers and sunshine—to grow up. Reading and heeding His Word, and prayer with service are tools of cultivation in your life. But here is another that might strike a responsive note.

"Do you want a change in your life? All it takes is 15 minutes a day." This is the title and lead-in to an article that came to me a couple of years ago. Let me quote from it: "What's the biggest dream of your life? How important is it? How much would you give up to make it happen? Here is an astoundingly true fact: You can do just about anything you want to do if you spend just 15 minutes a day at it.

"In three years you can become an expert on any subject you care to study—Chinese art, computer programming, cooking, bricklaying, gardening—if you work at it 15 minutes a day.

"In a year or less you could—
read the entire Bible
plant and keep up a small garden
become physically fit
learn to play a musical instrument
paint a house
learn a foreign language

write a book (the list is limitless).

"My first project was to tackle a badly neglected flower garden which was choked with weeds. Every time I looked out the dining room window, I fretted, because I thought I had no time whatever to try to redeem that impossible garden.

"Then I learned how many weeds I could pull in 15 minutes! It took just one week, snatching a quarter hour here, another there, to get that flower border tidy and ready for new transplants.

"The beauty of 15 minutes a day is that it helps me to stop postponing those things I really want or need to do and get them under way. It halts procrastination and banishes discouragement."[4]

The writer of the article, Charlotte Hale Allen, reports that women suggest these 15-minute package projects: help a child tidy a room; make a beautiful dessert; take a short walk; straighten a wardrobe closet; read books; take a bubble bath; phone an older person; listen to God; write a note; do something special for a family member . . .

Be a farmer who cultivates a productive life in Christ and accepts each day—with all its quarter hours—as a gift from God.

Cultivate a thankful heart. Count your blessings!

## There Is a Time for Weeding

"When the wheat sprouted and formed heads, then the weeds also appeared" (Matt. 13:26). Weeds sap strength from the soil. Weeds demand nourishment and get it from the food for the growing-up plant. Weeds are worthless.

Weeding is necessary to keep out those things which would sap the energy and nourishment necessary for the growth of the good seedling. Weeding will keep them from taking hold and choking out the life which is unto fruitfulness.

Weeding is also your part. "Get rid of all that is wrong in your life," James 1:21 states (*TLB*) too clearly for comfort! We are responsible to weed out.

There's one thing I'd like to ask You, Lord.
> It has puzzled me often:
> why do weeds grow easier than
> flowers?

I see it right before my eyes:
> I sow flowers and produce weeds.
> I sow grass and raise crabgrass;
my frail plants are choked by luscious dandeli-
> ons.

Now I have no personal animosity against dan-
> delions, Master.
> They are bright, cheerful flowers.
> Sensible too,
> for they shut up at night,
> which is more than many people do.
But why should dandelions that I don't plant
> thrive better than the flowers I protect?

How is it that from a packet of choice seeds
> all I get is chickweed?

If it were only a question of flowers and weeds
> it would be strange enough,
> but the tendency goes further and
> deeper.
> I find it within my own being,
> a downward pull,
> a gravitation to a lower level.

It is a daily fight to keep the standard high,
> to bring forth flowers instead of weeds,

> good instead of evil
> in my life, character and service.
>
> Lord, is it a law in your moral world,
>     as well as in your natural world,
>     that the more valuable the product
>     the harder it is to produce?[5]

If you promise not to tell my musician husband, I will sing a little song that I learned when I was about five, with motions that you are going to have to picture—especially the bunny part!

> Root them out, get them gone
> All the little bunnies in the field of corn,
> Envy, jealous, malice and pride,
> All if allowed in my heart would abide!

There are lists of *weeds* in the Scripture, and this one comes from Galatians 5. In the audacious paraphrase of *The Living Bible*, this list comes just a little too close to my "garden": "But when you follow your own wrong inclinations your lives will produce these evil results: impure thoughts, eagerness for lustful pleasure, idolatry, spiritism (that is, encouraging the activity of demons), hatred and fighting, jealousy and anger, constant effort to get the best for yourself, complaints and criticisms, the feeling that everyone else is wrong except those in your own little group—and there will be wrong doctrine, envy, murder, drunkenness, wild parties, and all that sort of thing. Let me tell you again as I have before, that anyone living that sort of life will not inherit the kingdom of God" (vv. 19-21).

Just in case you cannot find any weeds in that list that have ever sprouted in your life, take a magnifying glass to Ephesians 4:25-29, or Colossians 3:5-9.

What is a farmer to do when weeds sprout their ugly

heads in spite of his best efforts?

First, what the servant-leader-farmer is not to do! Never, never, never think you can coexist with that spiritual-energy-sapping weed. It will do you in every time! Soon even the most innocuous weed will spurt growth and cut off the sun and showers from the growing plant. With the direct access to sunlight cut off, the plant can soon forget that maturity unto fruitbearing was that for which the seed was first sown.

Do not let your influence as a leader be marred by the presence of pettiness, envy, malice or pride.

Do agree with God that these things are in fact SIN and all get weeded out. Since the weeds have no attachment to the vine or branches, it ought not to hurt to remove them. Ponder that a bit, before we move to the fourth step in the cultivation of a Christian, the pruning.

### There Is a Time for Pruning

At last we have come to God's part. Pruning is often painful but productive, and is the work of the Gardener. "He cuts off every branch in me that bears no fruit, while every branch that does bear fruit he trims clean so that it will be even more fruitful. You are already clean because of the word I have spoken to you" (John 15:3).

Please don't confuse the weeding and the pruning processes. "Why is God doing this to me? Why is God letting this happen in my life?"

Some of the things that are hurting us are simply a result of our own sin. We are responsible to see that weeds are removed by our choice and confession. The Lord will not sow sin in your life so that you can experience the pain of pruning. Negative, confusing attitudes or actions are not sown into your leadership by the Gardener of your heart! Those are weeds. As you take another look at John 15, you will note that it is only grown-up, mature, fruitbearing branches that are able to be pruned.

We were driving through the Fresno Valley of California last fall and saw acre upon acre of grape stumps. The vinedressers had gone up and down the rows lopping off the vines that had been dragging to the ground with succulent bunches of grapes hardly any time before.

It takes a while for the newly planted grapevines to grow to that fruitbearing stage before they can stand the lopping off process. What care and training are required before the farmer prunes "back for greater strength and usefulness" (John 15:3, *TLB*). His harvest is at stake, and he knows what he is doing.

Is God allowing circumstances, associations, testing to enter your life according to His timing, to increase your strength?

Joni Eareckson has experienced pruning in her life. In the most recent movie of her life, in which she testifies to the sustaining power of God as she has learned to adapt to being a quadraplegic, Joni is a powerful witness. As she speaks to thousands on the platform of a Billy Graham Crusade she is able to say that were she to have to trade what God has come to mean to her through the "tragedy" of losing the use of her limbs, for the ability to become upright and independent of her wheelchair, she would not be able to do it. Greater strength and usefulness—Joni has been pruned back.

Joni has opened a ministry in Southern California for handicapped persons. There is no way to count the lives that have been influenced to Christ or have been encouraged to trust God through her spirit-fruitbearing. She recognizes, however, that most probably her life is far more useful to the Lord than it ever could have been had she been allowed to pursue the "normal" young American girl pattern.

Think about that which pricks your pride. Those thorns that are so troublesome to you. Are the things which are hurting you now relating to weeds or can you accept those painful circumstances as part of God's pruning in your life because you have been forgiven up to date of all known sin?

Pruning is an indication of loving care to make you into His useful, productive person. The Lord Jesus cares about you and your service to Him. He has placed inestimable value upon you, and it is His plan that you should "[attain] to the whole measure of the fullness of Christ" (Eph. 4:13).

Dr. E. Stanley Jones has written these words: "A Christian yielded to God and His work within uses his pains, sets them to music, makes them sing. Every jolt only jolts the glory out. Every kick only kicks him forward. Even if he stumbles, he stumbles forward. He is like the apple trees which had especially fine apples on them. When asked the reason, the owner pointed to the slashes on the trunk of the tree, saying, 'For some reason the trees bear better fruit when slashed and wounded in this way. So we slash them into added fruitfulness.' "

Grow up so that God can begin to really shape your life. If He will, allow Him to prune you through disciplines in your leadership. J.B. Phillips has translated Hebrews 12:11 like this: "But God corrects us all our days for our own benefit, to teach us his holiness. Now obviously no 'chastening' seems pleasant at the time: it is in fact most unpleasant. Yet when it is all over we can see that it has quietly produced the fruit of real goodness in the characters of those who have accepted it in the right spirit."

So take a fresh grip on life.

## There Is a Time for Harvesting

In the fullness of His timing, fruit is produced. Depend upon it! Let your concentration be upon the abiding. "If [anyone] remains in me and I in him, he will bear much fruit" (John 15:5). We have been chosen to produce fruit.

A pathetic part of Scripture to me is Isaiah 5:1-6:

I will sing for the one I love
    a song about his vineyard:
My loved one had a vineyard
    on a fertile hillside.
He dug it up and cleared it of stones
    and planted it with the choicest vines.
He built a watchtower in it
    and cut out a winepress as well.
Then he looked for a crop of good grapes,
    but it yielded only bad fruit.

Now you dwellers in Jerusalem and men of
    Judah,
    judge between me and my vineyard.
What more could have been done for my vine-
    yard
    than I have done for it?
When I looked for good grapes,
    why did it yield only bad?

Now I will tell you
    what I am going to do to my vineyard:
I will take away its hedge,
    and it will be destroyed;
I will break down its wall,
    and it will be trampled.

I will make it a wasteland,
    neither pruned nor cultivated,
    and briers and thorns will grow there.
I will command the clouds
    not to rain on it."

Do you picture the Saviour-Sower laboring to provide the best possible conditions for growing and reaping a harvest of fine fruit? Can you hear the pathos when no crop is realized, "What more could have been done?"

Is it too harsh to suggest that God ought to be able to see more fruit from His farmer-leaders' lives? From our ministries?

The Bible suggests that there are several kinds of fruit that the Christian can and should be producing. Here are just a few:

"Fruit of *righteousness* that comes through Jesus Christ—to the glory and praise of God" (Phil. 1:11, italics added).

"Fruit in *every good work*, growing in the knowledge of God" (Col. 1:10, italics added).

"Fruit of the *Spirit* . . . love, joy, peace, patience, kindness, goodness, faithfulness, gentleness and self-control" (Gal. 5:22,23, italics added). This is the fruit of Christian character.

"Let us continually offer to God a sacrifice of *praise*— the fruit of lips that confess his name" (Heb. 13:15, italics added).

We are identified by the fruit we bear! What commends a certain apple tree to you? The sight of big red apples on its branches! Wish I had the nerve to say to some folks I meet what was said by someone braver than I from a pulpit one day: I would believe in your Redeemer if you looked more redeemed!

Never having heard a conversation I am not able to say whether or not she talked with her plants. But I do know that my "mother-in-love" could make things grow! Her green thumb was so powerful that it would make the thumb of the Jolly Green Giant look like Thumbelina. The final count in their home was 86 live plants—each one reminiscent of special people and special places.

Mother and Dad traveled widely on preaching missions, and mother was not above pulling one leaf off a particularly smashing plant, wrapping it carefully in wet Kleenex and—dumping hairpins from the baggie in her purse—placing it in the baggie so it would continue incubating until they got home. She had plants miraculously

growing in her California backyard that formerly had
lived in an African village. Blooming plants in San Jose
that had crossed the ocean as a leaf in a wad of wetness
from Sweden.

At the least sign of interest, Mother would introduce
you to the plant—or at least relate its (pardon the pun)
family tree. She just plain knew about growing things.

Dad was left in charge of the greenery when Mother
was taken to the hospital. His care and feeding of the
plants was something less than the personal attention
given by the lady-farmer of the house.

He simply removed them all to the lush but sunny
center of the backyard and hosed them all down. Yes,
violets and verbena, palms and pansies, all got the same
treatment. Dad had a few things to learn about growing
things and their special needs.

God, the Master Gardener, is to be thanked for His
special, careful consideration for our uniqueness. He sees
us as individuals, growing, and capable of producing
fruit.

### There Is a Time for Feasting

"The hardworking farmer should be the first to
receive a share of the crops" (2 Tim. 2:6).

I guess I have always envied a bit those farmers' wives
who have fresh vegetables on their table at every meal,
and their freezers full before Thanksgiving, and that old
fashioned fruit cellar lined with glass jars of tomatoes,
pickles and peaches. But I think I am like the little boy
who, when asked what he wanted to be when he grew
up, replied, "Either a returned veteran, a retired missionary, or a plantation owner." I would like to be a farmer
after the harvest. If there was only some way to short-cut
the hard work involved.

One of the happy by-products of serving Christ as a
farmer-leader is the opportunity to enjoy the firstfruits.
Who do you think is receiving the maximum benefit from

this book? ME! Of course. God is making me dig in, think through, write out, and make certain of all that you are reading. The teacher is the best taught, the leader is most thoroughly blessed; the reward is the greatest for the one who has invested the most time and effort.

As a matter of fact, unless you are getting fed yourself and being enriched and nourished through your study and preparation, you will not be effective in feeding others.

Be a farmer who is the first to enjoy the fruit of your labor in leadership.

There are some things a farmer-leader does that are significant to her ministry.

*A farmer plows.* I am not certain about this but I think there are two reasons why a farmer plows: first, to turn over the soil that has not been used for planting before and break up the crust; second, to plow back into the ground those stems and roots left there after the harvest has been gathered.

"Break up your unplowed ground and do not sow among thorns" (Jer. 4:3). A farmer realizes that the fallow, crusted ground must be turned over. It must be prepared. In your ministry you must be careful to prepare the soil before you sow seed willy-nilly among thorns. Before you even consider launching into a new ministry in a new area, prepare the area with the hardest work you can do—prayer.

Or perhaps, after a particularly rich time of harvest, you need to pull back and plow under with prayer before a new planting is made.

*A farmer invests.* Any farmer worth his salt invests; he won't just look out the farmhouse window, surveying endless acreage, and decide to go the route of least effort. "There is so much risk involved. Think what might happen if a hailstorm were to blow across the land come midsummer. The safe way is simply to make the smallest possible investment just in case. I don't think I will plant too much this year."

If you would reap a harvest, you will have to invest the most and the best that you can.

This think-small attitude usually strikes the church women's ministries about springtime. It is worse than spring fever! You have worked hard all fall and winter, planned meetings, recruited "farmhands" to be on kitchen committees, served at receptions, and made certain the nursery workers' roster was filled for both services. Summer cannot come soon enough for you, and as you think about the fall and the salad supper to get everybody rallied again, you almost yield to temptation. "Let's not get so involved next year. Let's not go to so much trouble. Let's cut the missions budget and we won't have to work so hard. Let's cut down the number of teachers' meetings, let's leave out—let's pare down—let's not go out on a limb—

The Scripture says, Whatever you sow is what you are going to reap. "And let us not get tired of doing what is right, for after a while we will reap a harvest of blessing if we don't get discouraged and give up" (Gal. 6:9, TLB).

It was the best potato crop anyone could remember. Mountains of potatoes! The legend says that all the villagers had potatoes on their tables every day. Baked, boiled, mashed—the biggest and best. They ate them raw, peeled or plain. They saved the scrubby ones for seeding and enjoyed the prize potatoes. A few years passed and the strangest thing happened to the potato crop, it shrunk! No more did they have big, meaty, snow-white potatoes. They had to be content with little brown bullet-size spuds. Why? Because they had sowed the leftovers for too long. If they wanted good, big potatoes, they were going to have to sow some good, big potatoes.

It is not quite the same in your ministry. God graciously multiplies and magnifies; but still we must invest our best in faith that He will increase it. Be one who spares nothing, holds nothing back, and you will enjoy the maximum harvest for your labors.

*A farmer cooperates with conditions.* A farmer doesn't plow in the dead of winter or doesn't sow in autumn. A farmer reads the almanac and plans the year's work. He is adaptable when adjustments must be made for unexpected weather changes. Be a farmer who is careful not to plow through established patterns and plans, who cooperates with God. "Peacemakers who sow in peace raise a harvest of righteousness" (Jas. 3:18).

Paul conveyed to the Corinthians that no one farmer is more important than another, and cooperation is the key to getting the job done. "My work was to plant the seed in your hearts, and Apollos' work was to water it, but it was God, not we, who made the garden grow in your hearts. The person who does the planting or water-ing isn't very important, but God is important because he is the one who makes things grow" (1 Cor. 3:6,7, *TLB*).

A retired businessman, with a latent desire to be a farmer, bought a plot of ground. He set to work clearing the rocky, overgrown soil, then planted the seed. What a job it turned out to be!

A preacher passed by one day as the man was stand-ing in the midst of his now-productive garden, pleasuring it. The preacher commented, in spiritual tones, "What a wonderful garden God has given you. You must be very thankful."

The man reflected, then replied, "Yes, but you should have seen it when God had it alone!"

We are God's co-workers; we cooperate with Him.

*A farmer expects a harvest.* By far the most important characteristic of a farmer is optimism. Picture a gardener, kneeling in the dirt, seeds all selected, trowel and water-ing can at hand. With every little hole dug he mutters, "It will never grow. I have never had any luck with plants. Impossible. The seeds don't look right. It probably is too sunny here. Or too shady. Or the neighbor's dog will choose this spot to bury his bone."

On a larger scale, can a farmer afford to expect disaster? Faith and risk go together just as surely as faith and work. Remember the verse we noted way back in the first pages—Psalm 42:11, "expect God to act"?

It was touch-and-go this last month for a small committee of women in San Jose. The chairman for the special interdenominational prayer breakfast had invested weeks of planning and prayer. The restaurant was reserved, the menu checked, the finances arranged, tickets printed, speakers and musicians contacted and arranged for. Several prayer times had been set just to focus on this one event. Just two weeks to go and only a handful of tickets had been sold.

"Audrey, when do you decide that this has gone far enough? It just won't work. It is only good business to face your limitations; you should cancel if you do not have at least 200 by this weekend."

No! Audrey would have none of it. To believe that the Lord was planning the direction for the breakfast and had particular purposes for this meeting required a belief that prayer would have an effect. God would act! And He did! Never have I seen Audrey so excited—well over 300 men and women came. The Lord met us there. She believed that it was God's way to do exceeding abundantly above all that we could ask or think, and either prayer and trust in God are the added dimension in a Christian's life and ministry or they are not.

Are you a servant-leader who expects the blessing of God on your ministry? On the investment of your time, your abilities, and your planning?

Be the farmer who has cooperated with the conditions, invested only your best, and trusted God for the increase.

### Cultivate a Committee

After you have recruited your committee, using scriptural principles, and have appointed one person to be responsible for each phase of your program, ministry or event, call a meeting of the committee. This must be a report session not a discussion time, else you will find yourself frustrated when the meeting is over and the last cup of coffee is drained. Your time will have been spent deciding on the flavor of cupcakes and the color of the invitations, rather than coordinating the decisions of the subcommittees who are to make those preliminary recommendations.

Following is a checklist of things you should do to prepare for a committee meeting:

☐ Secure the room or place of meeting. Clear the meeting through the church office to be sure it makes it to the church calendar.

☐ Announce to each committee member the time, date, place of meeting, either by mail or phone—or both.

☐ Prepare and duplicate an agenda because—

—it will help you stay on target and allow everyone to see the kinds and number of items to be discussed.

—it will help you gauge your timing. One superintendent I know prepares the agenda with the time estimate for each item in the left margin.

—it sometimes negates the need for minutes as each one notes on her own agenda sheet the ideas and decisions that are shared.

—it creates accountability. Each member is responsible to the rest of her committee for her homework.

—it is a tangible way to emphasize the need for prayer—providing a list of things that need to be prayed for. The agenda could be printed on colored paper or stationery and have an emblem or decorative seal in the corner.

☐ Decorate your meeting area. Use this as an opportunity to make the setting conducive to business. There is a ministry in a bowl of flowers, pretty napkins, tiny favors. Obviously, it is a signal that "you have been prepared for." It tends to communicate that something very important is about to happen.

☐ Plan refreshments. Now some people don't like "eatin meetins' " but simple, pretty refreshments enhance fellowship, I think. Ever consider sharing a recipe as part of your agenda? Since most people do not arrive together, it is my suggestion that your committee meetings are conducted around a table, or tables, and the refreshments are available as the women arrive and are seated.

☐ Allow for only six or seven minutes of settling in, pouring coffee, and conversation before you go to work on that agenda; begin with a time with the Lord (led by one who has previously been asked to do so).

Have you ever been part of a committee that weeps when the event is over? Make your committee service unforgettable: a time to build and deepen fellowship, to learn to appreciate each other's gifts and abilities. Discover that this sisterhood of believers is a serendipity of service.

Never forget, however, that there are still those women in each organization for whom Robert's Rules of Order will never go out of style. Can I slip in an experience that really has nothing whatever to do with farming?

It was a Friday afternoon near Christmas. Wanting to express how important the guild meeting was to which I had been invited to speak, I donned a long, red and green dress and *slipped* all the way to the church on the icy Minneapolis streets. The aroma of coffee cake and coffee, mixed with fresh greenery, met each woman who entered the festive fellowship hall.

Those of us who were part of the program sat semicircle around a large desk up front. The chairman pounded her gavel (perhaps she didn't really have a gavel—it just seemed like she did!) and called this Christmas meeting to order. While we were all eyeing the calorie-laden buffet tables, and nearly drifting into that cozy after-lunch-early-afternoon euphoria common to afternoon women's meetings, the chairman called for the minutes!

The secretary stood, opened her book and began: "The Women's Guild Board meeting, held on such and such a date, did such and such things, including the decision to recommend to the guild at large the following— The following—"

Panic! The secretary leafed through pages of minutes—all those records of monumental decisions gone by, all those laboriously worded edicts and *she couldn't find the recommendation*. What could she do? With face burning—or was it just the wavering glow of the candle-light—she dashed from the room. We sang a snatch of a Christmas carol, and then the kitchen door flew open and she emerged to take her place in her secretary's chair again.

Whew! How glad we were that the lost had been found—but what did it say? You won't believe this, but cross my heart and hope to die it was true!

"The Board of the Women's Guild makes this recommendation—that we dispense with all business at the Christmas tea!"

The vote was taken, and after it was moved, seconded, and voted upon, we dispensed with the business. Minutes are necessary, but let them not be read at every meeting. Nearly 10 minutes of prime time was spent on that irrelevant "piece of business."

You will be warmly remembered if you are a committee chairman who makes your meetings occasions, and keeps them report sessions, not discussion groups.

The country person had this idea for a productive garden. Can you see how it could be a launching agenda for a committee meeting? Your centerpieces could be baskets of vegetables; refreshments, raw vegetables with a special dip, served with crackers.

First, plant five rows of peas—Preparedness, Promptness, Perseverance, Politeness and Prayer.

Next to them plant three rows of squash: Squash indifference, Squash gossip and Squash criticism.

Then five rows of lettuce: Let us be faithful, Let us be truthful, Let us be unselfish, Let us be loyal, Let us love one another.

And no garden is complete without turnips: Turn up for church, Turn up with a smile, Turn up with a new idea, Turn up with determination.

### Cultivating a Resource File

Are you the person who has a place for everything and everything in its place? Then stop reading—this next part is for those of us with our kitchen drawers all junk drawers, with dresser drawers stuffed with memorable notes, bookmarks, and old programs; whose glove compartments are full of last week's and last year's Sunday bulletins (too pretty to toss), and last but not least, a garage overflowing with Christmas cards, birthday cards, and get-well cards from your first surgery. Need I say more? Some of us are pack rats. I cannot remember the last time I read or saw something that I did not consider recycling either in a conversation or a craft!

At last, a system to help you get organized!

Here is a way you can create a resource file or weed out a lot of things you want to keep.

1. Assemble the following materials: manila folders as needed; 8½-by-11-inch paper; all the clippings you wish to save on any and all subjects.

2. On each 8½-by-11-inch piece of paper glue or tape the articles to be filed. Attach as many as will fit on each sheet regardless of subject or topic. Use only one side of each paper.

3. Number each 8½-by-11-inch sheet of clippings in the upper right corner consecutively. Place papers numbered 1-25 in the first folder. As you continue to add material that you gather, prepare it the same way. The next folder will contain pages numbered 26-50; then 51-

75; etc.

4. Beginning with the first page of clippings, #1: write across the top of a three-by-five inch card a subject heading appropriate to the first article on sheet #1. Under this first general topic, put #1.

That article might be more easily located if you also cross-reference it under an alternate heading. So make another three-by-five card on the alternate topic as well, also listing #1 on it. Perhaps you might need up to three cards, with three different headings for that one article.

If there are other clippings on page #1, repeat the procedure for each subject or heading on three-by-five cards. Follow through with all your pages of clippings, recording on the appropriate card the page number where the article is found.

5. Let's have a go at it again:
   a. Collect all your stuff. -
   b. While watching television or coffee-ing with a neighbor tape all your wonderful stuff onto 8½-by-11-inch sheets of paper.
   c. Almost without thinking, do it, and then number the pages in the top right corner. Don't get confused because of all you have learned about filing before! Just put lots of different subjects on the same page.
   d. At some other time—maybe on vacation—get out your three-by-fives and open the first folder (all you need to take with you when you tracle according to subject, always remembering to note the page number on the card that applies to that subject.
   e. Now when you have to give a two-minute motivational message, you go to your three-by-five card file, look under FARMER or MOTIVATION or OPTIMISM and you will find just the page number you need to locate the article you want.

6. Following is a clipping that "just fits." (You better copy it or type it onto another piece of paper so you don't have to cut up this book, or you will never remember these instructions!)

### Hurrah for the Hen!!

Hard work means nothing to a hen. She just keeps on digging worms and laying eggs regardless of what the business prognosticators say about the outlook for this or any other year. If the ground is hard, she scratches harder. If it is dry, she digs deeper. If it's wet, she digs where it's dry. If she strikes a rock, she works around it. If she gets a few more hours of daylight, she gives us a few more eggs—but she always digs up worms and turns them into hard-shelled profits as well as tender, profitable broilers. Did you ever see a pessimistic hen? Did you ever hear of one starving to death waiting for worms to dig themselves up? Did you ever hear one cackle because work was hard? Not on your life!! They save their breath for digging and their cackles for eggs. Success means digging! Are you digging?

**Notes**
1. Lloyd John Ogilvie, *Autobiography of God* (Ventura, CA: Regal Books, 1979), p. 56.
2. Ibid., pp. 57-59.
3. Ibid., p. 62.
4. Charlotte Hale Allen, *Power Magazine*, 1979.
5. Flora Larsson, "Weeds and Flowers," *Just a Moment, Lord* (Wheaton, IL: Harold Shaw, 1974), p. 73.

## Seven

# The Workman

"Work hard so God can say to you, 'Well done.' Be a good workman, one who does not need to be ashamed when God examines your work. Know what his Word says and means" (2 Tim. 2:15, *TLB*).

It all takes place in a carpenter shop. The tools are having an argument and the hammer is up front, trying to call for order. "Things need to be changed around here!" The hammer raises his voice above the din. "There are problems needing to be solved. We have got to get the work done, and I have thought of a solution: We must get rid of some of the troublemakers. As a matter of fact, we can do without the saw. The saw only makes a mess, and this shop would be better off without him."

The saw hears the hammer's words about how they need to clean up and is quick to answer, "Just a minute; the hammer is the one who is always flying off the handle around here. All he does is pound, pound, pound, driving home his point. I think we could well do without him."

The wrench hears the argument, and as usual opens his mouth to add fuel to the fight.

The saw retorts, "Yes, you too, wrench, you know you have the biggest mouth around this shop and we all want you to leave!"

The wrench, when it has the chance, says, "I know I have problems but they are nothing compared to those of the measure. That measure has one standard, and it is its own. It measures everything and everybody by itself. Couldn't we do without the measure.?"

"The plane can go anytime," says the measure. "It has no depth to anything it does. Skims only the surface of the situation—all superficial." The plane hears it all and pushes the chisel to the center of the floor and adds, "I may not be the most useful tool in this shop, but the chisel just takes pleasure in digging. Dig, dig, dig, in every situation. Seems to delight in hurting others. Never misses an opportunity to get that one more dig in."

"All right, fellas, I know I have a bit of a personality problem, but do you realize that the file is only good for one thing too—to rub things the wrong way? We would have a little peace in the shop if it weren't for the file."

Into the shop roll a couple of nuts. "Hi, fellas, what's going on?" As they hear the argument they are quick to join in with, "Go on and argue, if you want to, but remember that we are what holds things together around here. We may be only little nuts but you couldn't do without us!"

Quiet up until now, the level finally says, "Actually, my good brothers, I guess I am the only one who is really on the level in this shop. Perhaps someday you will understand and realize my dependability."

What a commotion! Suddenly the door swings open and a pile of wood lumbers into the shop and, when it lays itself in a pile on the floor, it says, "Go ahead, go to work on us. We know that every time we come in here you have a different idea about what we ought to be. You seem to think that we need to be made over—so go to it." Discouraged, the wood just lays there.

Clump, clump, clump—in comes the sawhorse with a sigh and says, "At last the burden-bearer in this shop has arrived. Everybody see these broad shoulders? Well, they were made to bear the burdens of all the rest of you." There was more than a note of self-pity in the tones of the sawhorse, and it prompts all kinds of responses from the rest of the tools.

They don't even stop for long when the door opens and the Carpenter of Nazareth Himself walks into the shop. There seems to be a holy hush however, when He puts on His work apron, and sits at the bench and goes about His task. He picks up one tool, and then another, and hums as He works. This goes on all day long, as the tools find themselves being used!

At the end of the day, as the sun casts a warm glow on the work of the Carpenter, the tools begin to wonder what it was they were being used to build. The hammer, with awe, announces to the others as he looks up toward the sky, "Why, we have been used to build a cathedral; a Temple for the Living God!"

Every accusation which the tools made about one another was absolutely true, yet, during the construction, not one tool was indispensable. As they ponder the work, one of them—perhaps the hammer—murmurs.

"Brethren, I perceive that we are laborers together with God" (see 1 Cor. 3:9).

We have just come home from Sunday evening church service. There the soloist sang words that reinforced that which I had written just before leaving for the gathering. "To be used of God, that is my desire . . . to be used of God," over and over again. A young couple was being commissioned to attend seminary. They would be challenged over and over again, as they were this evening, to fulfill their ministry. The pastor read from 2 Timothy 2 about being a workman that doesn't need to be ashamed. Paul reinforces in his letters and his imagery that we are laborers, builders, workmen *and* the tools themselves. "Do not let any part of your bodies become tools of wickedness, to be used for sinning; but give yourselves completely to God—every part of you—for you are back from death and you want to be tools in the hands of God, to be used for his good purposes" (Rom. 6:13, *TLB*).

God is both Architect and Carpenter and He will use any of us hammers and saws to build.

### Be a Workman/Leader—One Who Builds

*The terms of the building contract:* "Let me show you what the man who comes to me, hears what I have to say, and puts it into practice, is really like. He is like a man building a house, who dug down to rock bottom and laid the foundation of his house upon it. Then when the flood came and the flood water swept down upon that house, it could not shift it because it was properly built." (Luke 6:48, *Phillips*).

*Consider the price:* "Suppose one of you wants to build a tower. Will he not first sit down and estimate the cost to see if he has enough money to complete it?" (Luke 14:28). Consider what it might cost you to be a subcontractor who is willing to work hard to build. You who have assumed any leadership roles at all will be shaking your heads loudly when the *prices* of being a workman-leader are discussed. There are costs to be contended with in serving the Lord—out front. One of those prices is in your vulnerability to criticism. In a few pages we will talk about that destructive critical spirit; but consider that and other costs in building the Kingdom.

Someone has said, have your tools ready and God will find you work! Although I believe it, I don't do it without risks.

*The guarantee:* "Then every workman who has built

on the foundation with the right materials, and whose work still stands, will get his pay" (1 Cor. 3:14, *TLB*).

*The contractor:* "Unless the Lord builds a house, the builders' work is useless" (Ps. 127:1, *TLB*).

> O Lord,
> You know how much I long to work for you—
> For you have done so much within the heart of
>     me.
> I must begin somewhere though talents may
>     seem few
> Because about me there are needs I see.
> Perhaps I've been a bit too timid, Lord,
> Afraid to reach, to touch another life through
>     mine.
> What joy that reaching, touching can afford
> When I join hands with Thee in work divine.
>                         (author unknown)

Many years ago at Mission Springs I heard Lila Trotman, the widow of Dawson Trotman, the founder of the Navigator movement, tell the story about how God had almost mystically allowed her husband to know that he was soon going to heaven. They were seated together by a lake and Dawson took the time to carefully tell her about how God had raised up the Navigator movement during the second World War, about its workings, and the plans for the future of the work.

The immediate responsibilities for leadership might fall on her shoulders.

Within two weeks Dawson drowned while trying to save another, and over and over it sobered her how God had prepared him in order that Dawson could prepare her.

Their home had always been the central location for fellowship and training. People were always around her table—because of their growing family and their burgeoning ministry. She had to come to grips with the management of their home and the responsibility of the ministry. Working with people without her husband's support, having to step into a situation that she didn't feel suited to, and at the same time handling her grief. How could she do it!

One of the disciplines she began was to read one chapter in the Bible seven times a day! She did not memorize it; she read it.

But there were moments of tension as the adjustments in the organization were made. Submitting herself to the shaping and molding of God in her own life, she was able to pray a simple, life-controlling prayer:

"Lord, let me never enter a life except to build!"

Except to build.

Do you affirm that this is a foundation prayer in the life of the Godly woman workman?

"By the grace God has given me, I laid a foundation as an expert builder, and someone else is building on it. But each one should be careful how he builds. For no one can lay any foundation other than the one already laid, which is Jesus Christ. If any man builds on this foundation using gold, silver, costly stones, wood, hay or straw, his work will be shown for what it is, because the Day will bring it to light. It will be revealed with fire, and the fire will test the quality of each man's work" (1 Cor. 3:10-13).

What nursery story does that remind you of? Right! The three little pigs! Remember how they set out to build their houses, and each bought the stuff to build with. First the straw, then the wood, and finally the smart little pig built his house of bricks. When the big bad wolf came to huff and to puff and to try to blow down the brick house, he was stymied and had to climb on the roof to come down through the chimney. He plopped right into the kettle of boiling water the wise little pig had waiting for him!

First Corinthians 3 tells us to be careful what we use

to build with—not wood, hay and stubble, but the precious stones that will last throughout eternity. The day will come when our work will be tried. Let us be sure not to be duped into thinking we can be a modern Miss Piggy who builds with stuff that just doesn't stand up to the onslaughts of the big bad wolf, for expediency. Be a workman that builds for the long haul, without shortcuts, who places bricks of Christian character, commitment to prayer and planning, bricks of love for the lost and poor. Wood, hay and stubble building is akin to the let's-have-a-dilly-of-a-program-this-year leadership pattern, that lacks purpose and goals and ministry.

Amy Carmichael was a teenager in Northern Ireland just a few years before she set out for the Orient to eventually become the founder of Dohnavur Fellowship in Southern India. It was a windy, damp day as Amy and her family were on their way home from church. Shocked to see an old woman in rags struggling with a heavy bundle, young Amy thought surely the woman should have been in church!

Suddenly Amy turned and ran after the older woman, took her by the arm, and carried the burden for her. The onlookers laughed to see this incongruous team, and Amy burned red with embarrassment. Misery threatened to engulf her—wet, sad, hurt and humiliated, the Spirit of God recalled 1 Corinthians 3:13 to her mind: "The fire shall try every man's work of what sort it is." A phrase came to her heart that was to be one of her life-mottoes: Nothing is important but that which is eternal.

Amy Carmichael, in her life's work of rescuing and serving India's temple children as well as in writing deep devotional books for building in the lives of millions, is a model of a workman who does not need to be ashamed! The praise or taunts of men are not worthy building materials. The favor of her heavenly Father, the knowledge of the approval of her Lord—these would be her motives and motivations.

Amy Carmichael would have been the last one to classify herself as a leader by the standards of this world, but a servant-leader, according to the principles of the Word of God, she surely was! She writes of calvary love in her classic volume *If*. It is not a book to be glanced at or read in one sitting, though it contains only several hundred words. It is a collection of thought and prayer-starters. Let me share one that "fits" right here: "If one whose help I greatly need appears to be as content to build in wood, hay, stubble, as in gold, silver, precious stones, and I hesitate to obey my light and do without that help because so few will understand, then I know nothing of Calvary love."[1]

There is often a loneliness in leadership; Amy Carmichael knew that loneliness but was never alone. Her work had been planned before the beginning of time for her, and nothing less than a lifelong commitment to building for eternity, regardless of the support or lack of it from those around her, was satisfactory!

What is the hard work that 2 Timothy 2:15 challenges us to do?

"Study and be eager and do your utmost to present yourself to God approved (tested by trial), a workman who has no cause to be ashamed, correctly analyzing and accurately dividing—rightly handling and skillfully teaching—the Word of Truth" (*AMP*).

That is a tall order! And work!

The work is the proper application of the Word of God. That is how I would like most to be introduced: as a W.O.W.! A woman of the Word.

Some of you in my age group—both physically and spiritually—have to admit that we have spent years and years in the Word. Some of us have attended (and/or taught) dozens, even hundreds, of Bible studies over the years. Some of us have even dared to regard our study of the Word as a spiritual safety-zone. It is comfortable to believe that when we are studying and reading we are

more spiritual than when we are washing dishes or playing tennis or serving on a phone committee for a coming
election.

That had better not be so! We are God's women
regardless of the activity or we are not God's women at
all. What I do does not make me more or less spiritual.
When I received Jesus as my Saviour and my resident,
live-in Lord, and the Holy Spirit came to dwell in me, my
life was opened up spiritually, and I became a spiritual
woman.

Bible study is not an end in itself, but a facilitator to
holy living. "Continue in what you have learned and
have become convinced of, because you know those
from whom you learned it, and how from infancy you
have known the holy Scriptures, which are able to make
you wise for salvation through faith in Christ Jesus. All
Scripture is God-breathed and is useful for teaching,
rebuking, correcting and training in righteousness, so that
the man of God may be thoroughly equipped for every
good work" (2 Tim. 3:14-17).

God has planned that His precious Word be *applied*
after thorough study and prayerful consideration.

In the middle verses of the nineteenth Psalm there are
six sections of three parts each that confirm the revelation
of God through His Word. The Scripture is titled six different ways, followed by an attribute of the Word, and
then how the Word of God should affect our lives.

| Title | Attribute | Effect |
|---|---|---|
| 7. The law of the Lord | is perfect, | reviving the soul. |
| The statutes of the Lord | are trust-worthy, | making wise the simple. |
| 8. The precepts of the Lord | are right, | giving joy to the heart. |
| The commands of the Lord | are radi-ant, | giving light to the eyes. |
| 9. The fear of the Lord | is pure, | enduring forever. |

The ordinances of the     are sure     and altogether
Lord                                    righteous.

As we use the Word in our lives and in our ministries, great care must be taken to make the applications in context. A sense of humor is a must as we hear of situations complicated by wrongly dividing the Word of truth.

A certain seven-year-old approached his father and said, "Daddy, when we sin we get smaller, don't we?"

"No," replied the dad. "Why do you say that?"

"Well," he exclaimed, "the Bible says, 'All have sinned and come short'!"

Or, a Sunday School teacher reported that the excuse the little girl gave for not having her memory work complete was "because the only copy of the Bible we have at home is the reversed version."

If you would be an approved workman-servant, you will want to have a systematic personal Bible study commitment. A resource guide for this time which is widely used is the *Daily Walk*, published by Walk Thru the Bible Ministries, Inc., P.O. Box 720653, Atlanta, Georgia 30358. It is a plan for reading the entire Bible through in a year. It is without a doubt the most helpful, complete, yet usable plan I have found. Several organizations and denominations as well as educational institutions in our nation have offered the *Daily Walk* through their own ministries.

Back to 2 Timothy 2.

"Keep reminding [people] of these things. Warn them before God against quarreling about words; it is of no value, and only ruins those who listen. . . . Avoid godless chatter, because those who indulge in it will become more and more ungodly" (2 Tim. 2:14,16).

Malettor Cross is a grand, black workman-servant, mother of 11 children. She and her husband Haman serve the Lord through their Detroit Afro-American Mission. It was a choice opportunity for me to meet her and then to get to know her as we shared a speaking assignment in northern Michigan.

She is introduced to you in a chapter in my book *Why Doesn't Somebody Do Something?*

"In our one-room church in Tennessee, four classes met in four corners, but the 'old folks' always got the choir loft. In that clapboard sanctuary I received the only Sunday School training I can remember.

" 'Okay, Brother, hear it again! "God who at sundry times in divers manners, spake in time past . . ."'

" 'Just a minute, Brother, you have talked too much. Let's hear from the preacher now!'

" 'Well, friends, let us consider this passage from another angle.

" ' "God, WHO AT SUNDRY TIMES AND IN DIVERS MANNERS SPAKE IN TIME PAST UNTO THE FATHERS BY THE PROPHETS, hath in these last days spoken unto us by His Son . . ." ' (Heb. 1:1, *KJV*).

"This was about as 'divers' a manner as God had ever spoken in, and I sat on the edge of my seat to listen to the outcome of the argument. Really it wasn't an argument, but a four-cornered pooling of ignorance. The winner was the loudest shouter.

"The only verse I can remember learning as a child is Hebrews 1:1. God has been dealing with me in 'divers' manners ever since I accepted Jesus as my Saviour when I was 11 years old."[2]

Malettor continued to share her fascinating pilgrimage with me, and her desire to rightly divide the Word without vain arguments. God is using her to do just that!

The Word is your tool. Use it not in useless haggling, but work hard to be worthy of the "well done." Essentially these verses tell us not to talk so much, and for some of us that is hard work.

"The good workman is true to the Scriptures. He does not falsify it. Nor does he try to confuse people, like Elymas the sorcerer, by 'making crooked the straight paths of the Lord.' (Acts 13:10). On the contrary, he handles the Word with such scrupulous care that he both stays on the path himself, keeping to the highway and avoiding the byways, and makes it easy for others to follow."[3]

## Life with Spice

Everybody should have the chance for the church's most creative job! *Program chairman* for the women's organization! I have had it several times and am going to write some books about it. Until then, let me tell you about a *Life with Spice*. These booklets have already been written.

The Lord gave an idea for *building* on the Word of God in some new ways in our neighborhood in South Minneapolis eight years ago. Using the theme of salts and seasonings from Matthew 5:13—"You are the world's seasoning, to make it tolerable. If you lose your flavor, what will happen to the world?" (*TLB*). Flyers of invitation were taken door to door around the church. It was below zero, and anyone in their right mind would not go out in a Minnesota January morning. A get-together for praying and preparing was planned at the church. The doors were opened. The sweet aroma of freshly-baked coffee cakes mingled with the perking tonic of a Scandinavian ministry (coffee). The quivery smiles on the faces of the dozen or so "workmen" greeted the 52 women and 27 children who entered Elim Covenant Church that morning.

The Word of God has been built upon in creative, challenging ways ever since. Lots of ingredients—good fellowship with neighbors, coffee and goodies, home-making ideas to reinforce the Word, exercises, gift and craft how-tos, prayer and time in the Scripture combined to make a ministry.

Because the Bible was given to equip us for every good work, not as a spiritual safety zone, the serendipity of our Life with Spice was beginning to see how appropriate the Scripture is to every area of our lives as women. Nine Bible study series have emerged from that beginning in 1973. Perhaps it would encourage you to act creatively, building on the Word, if you wrote and let me send you a sample.* Then you can use these, or create your own. Learn to use a topical concordance as well as resources to be found in your Christian bookstore.

Practice brainstorming creative get-togethers around the Scripture. Every part of your gathering can confirm the Word—the decorations, the menu, the focus or speaker as well as the study time. Design your meeting around tables; this plan provides a small group for discussion, fellowship, and brief study. Following is just one idea that has worked.

### Wings

A Christian airline pilot was to give his testimony to a mixed group in an evening get-together. Since involvement with the Scripture is a means to a deeper application, we always build in an opportunity for everyone to at least open their Bibles—or ones supplied—to confirm the message of the evening and its theme. Let me give you the program outline and the brief Bible study that was used that evening.

*Publicity:* Two uniformed "air line attendants" distributed "tickets" in the church narthex for two Sunday mornings before the meeting. We also distributed announcement flyers throughout the neighborhood.

*Decorations:* Tables were covered with white paper. Model airplanes and plants were centerpieces. Napkins and cups and plates were secured from a local airline.

*Refreshments:* Cabin attendants distributed packets of peanuts and took beverage orders. Several kinds of pie were served.

*Program:*

1. Welcome—as if on board a 747, complete with

safety features and exits. Introduction of pilots and attendants.

2. Prayer

3. Music—including the singing of this old poem to the tune of "What a Friend We Have in Jesus":

Said the robin to the sparrow, I should really
like to know
Why these anxious human beings, rush about
and worry so.

Said the sparrow to the robin, I think it sure
must be,
That they have no heavenly Father such as
cares for you and me.

4. Refreshments served by cabin attendants.

5. Everybody makes a paper airplane—and a distance race is held!

6. Bible study around individual tables—about 12 minutes.

In the Scripture, *Wings* are often mentioned. God teaches us lessons through birds and wings. Look up these verses and decide which words—all beginning with the letter *P*—best typify what these *wings* mean to us: Genesis 8:10 *P* _____ Isaiah 40:31 *P* _____ Matthew 6:26 *P* _____ Song of Solomon 2:12 *P* _____

7. Music—perhaps singing Isaiah 40:31, or special music.

8. Now—fasten seat belts and listen to the pilot—speaker.

Try the same outline with such topics as "Spiritual Fitness," or "The Time of Your Life," or "Lost and Found" (Luke 15).

## The Critic

A good thing to remember

A better thing to do
Work with the construction gang
Not with the wrecking crew![4]

Perhaps you will find this difficult to believe, but in three short days recently I was criticized three times! All unfounded remarks, of course—not one person had earned the right to criticize.

Something unsettling, even highly disturbing took place in my mind. At least I think it was in my mind. I reacted violently to these who dared to pass judgment on how I spent my time, my money, and right on down to a comment on my appearance! My reaction was the unsettling part. Being a "mature Christian woman" it was definitely out of character for me to respond to criticism with a critical spirit of my own.

There were moments when I wish I had never had stamped on my heart Lila Trotman's prayer, "Let Me Never Enter a Life Except to Build." There were no two ways about it—I was not building. I was cooperating with the demolition squad, the wrecking crew.

A critical spirit is so easily developed—almost accidentally. Women who are willing to take the risks of leadership must be on guard against this most destructive personal characteristic.

A good friend and prayer partner seemed so able to deal with this in her life. She was in the most vulnerable position of the pastor's wife. In prayer times with her, how often I recall her sincere petition: "Lord, please forgive my tendency to a critical spirit. Cleanse me from any shadow of a critical attitude, that I might serve Thee blamelessly."

Pondering this resurfacing character flaw of mine, a pattern was revealed as to how such a critical spirit is formed—and entrenched. Can you relate to these five steps?

Each of them begin with "I"—not exactly a surprise

since it is that overwhelming protection of *self* which is the core of most of our problems.

1. *Insecurity.* Whenever I begin to evaluate myself and get involved with destructive introspection, I open myself up to all manner of vain imaginations. "Why am I not better looking?" "If only I had more ability, or more money, or a charming ease with people!" Some of those things we have at least some control over, but so much that makes us insecure is beyond our control. We shake our fists in the face of God, complaining that He made some mistakes when He made us as we are.

If our security is to be in Christ, freeing us from an undue preoccupation with self, then is not insecurity a rebuke to God?

2. *Intimidation.* The creeping, crawly, critical spirit has this second step in its development.

Nehemiah was a builder. No sooner had he arrived in Jerusalem to begin the building project than Sanballat and Tobiah became insecure and stirred up trouble. They had been given a job to do and they had not done it. Do we fall into that trap? "Either I cannot or I won't do this job, but I don't want anyone more willing or qualified to do it either!"

Tobiah and Sanballat stood and watched (see Neh. 4:2) the people who had a mind to work. The workers were organized and were carrying bricks. They saw a need and under Nehemiah's leadership they were filling it. Tobiah and Sanballat were intimidated by the success of the effort. Are you ever intimidated by another's success?

"She does everything so well, I won't even try!"

"I could never do as well—or look as good—or say it as cleverly."

I may as well admit it to you, there are people in my life who intimidate me!

A few years ago I was speaking at a conference in the

East. I was in grand company—my sister-speaker is a great woman of God, and well-known and magnificently used by the Lord even internationally. What a privilege to become acquainted with her and other leaders at the retreat.

Several hundred women sat in front of me during that first session, and I felt the Lord just lift the hearts of all of us. He was doing just what He said He would do.

At a pre-retreat dinner with the leaders and visiting seminar leaders, three ladies from a nearby state, also with a very influential, successful ministry in retreats with women, shared about their continuing need for speakers. The three women sat in the fourth row during the general sessions, and as I was waxing eloquent during my second opportunity at the podium, my eyes were drawn to them. They were whispering. Then they wrote a note or two. I knew what they were doing! They were evaluating me— and what I was saying! I just knew they were deciding whether or not I was good enough.

*Intimidation*—that crippled my communication. Once I allowed my mind to be clouded and cluttered with the response of the three to me, my ability to communicate the message God had given to the 697 others was a zilch! Let me be quick to add that I was not the only one to notice it, and, there has not been an invitation to speak to that particular group! But my reaction disgusted me.

I want to react as Nehemiah did when he was intimidated by his opponents—snide remarks about the workers' inability to do the job and how foolish they looked trying to clear away the rubble to get to the construction site. Nehemiah sent one of his famous arrow prayers to the Lord, and kept right on building! He knew that he was responsible only for his own attitude, not the attitude or actions of others.

Well, I moved right along to the next step to reinforcing that critical spirit—

3. *Insinuation*. I blamed those women for my behav-

ior! Yes, I subtly but firmly transferred the responsibility. At this point no one else has to know what is happening; it can be like a game: "If they had not done this, I wouldn't have done that!" "If she weren't so short and cute, I wouldn't look so tall and awkward!" "If she were not such a great speaker, I would sound better!" "If my husband were as supportive as her husband, of course I would be better able to serve!"—You could keep right on going, couldn't you, with all sorts of personal examples— TELL ME YOU COULD!

How easily we can make ourselves believe that another's actions are responsible for our response.

4. *Insult*. There is that *I* again. Now I can begin to actually *see* that person or persons negatively. I get ready for the negative attitude about whatever is said, done, worn or, in some cases, even *eaten* by that person. That preparation for the negative, is often nothing more than *self-protection*.

Barbara is a person to be avoided by me. It is apparent that somehow and in some way I have intimidated her. I know you are laughing—how could anybody be intimidated by Daisy??? But Barbara has the uncanny ability to come up with negative questions—negative answers—and negative observations about me. "How are you doing, Daisy?"—an innocent enough question, right? If I let her in a bit on what occupies my days, her reply might be, "How does your husband feel about your being out of the house?" or, "You should treat yourself to a day off to get your hair done."

She is the type that, when you are as Nehemiah was—involved in a great project—can say, "I hope you won't have to neglect your home now," or "I know that this year's retreat is going to go much better than last!"

Immediately, flashing across my mind comes last year's great project, and try as I will, I cannot find what was so bad about it!

It is the better part of wisdom to prepare yourself for

*negative* "input" as a means of self-preservation when those encounters are expected.

Rate the following comments. Put a *D* in front of those you think might be Destructive, and *C* for Constructive:

_____ 1. "Do you know what we could do next year—instead?"

_____ 2. "Thank you for letting the Lord use you."

_____ 3. "I really enjoyed the banquet. Now remember that when you hear the criticisms."

_____ 4. "You really look tired!"

_____ 5. You certainly look better than the last time I saw you!"

_____ 6. "May I help you by praying for you?"

_____ 7. "Considering you had so little to work with, you have done a great job!"

Then there are those strictly personal comments: "I didn't know you sewed!" when you have just spent three weeks trying to make the latest outfit look store-bought. "I tried that blouse on, but it just didn't look like it was well made, so I didn't get it." "Do you enjoy wearing a wig?" My friend told me her husband calls this back-door complimenting "damnation by faint praise."

This step is reinforced in my attitude when I insult the other person or persons by looking for the point of vulnerability and magnifying it. "She has given this same message hundreds of times—how can it be thought to be careful preparation?" "Here she is talking about children, and I happen to know hers are no angels." "She doesn't even sew—she just has all the money in the world to buy her clothes."

But the last step is certainly the most destructive to the Kingdom.

5. *Influence others.* "Evil words destroy. Godly skill rebuilds" (Prov. 11:9, *TLB*).

A critical spirit is destructive in my own life, but when

gossip and criticism are shared with others—I enter lives to *destroy*. Gossip is sometimes disguised as *discernment*. Let me give you an outrageous example.

You have just attended a symphony concert. In the party afterward, someone launches a conversation, "Well, how did you like Beethoven tonight?" Balancing your 7-Up and petit-four, you venture, "I thought it was wonderful! The music was powerfully and movingly performed, don't you think?"

Then it happens. "I thought it was good, but of course, not nearly as well done as their last season in London. The cello section seemed to be out of tune, and the percussion just a bit weak . . ."

How do you feel? Like an unsophisticated know-nothing, correct? If you were up on Beethoven you would have been able to discern more of the error.

Or, you have just come from church. You say, "Wasn't that a grand service?"

"I don't think it was all that great. Didn't you notice how many mistakes the organist made?"

"Well, no, I guess I am not a musician, since I didn't notice that."

"And you didn't hear that prayer? If that was not self-righteous, I don't know what it was."

That critical spirit has taken the joy from me. There is a kind of pseudo-sophistication felt even in the church of Jesus Christ that surfaces in name-dropping in Christian circles and in armchair criticism of church leaders.

Let us not be foolish and say that discernment is not only necessary, but is a gift of God to enrich and empower our spiritual lives. Wisdom in sharing discernment goes hand-in-hand with the use of that spiritual gift.

Women of God, let our prayer be for forgiveness for any critical spirit that begins with a feeling of insecurity. That vulnerability leads to being intimidated because others do so well. "If she didn't do so well, I wouldn't show up so poorly," says the one who insinuates that the other person is somehow responsible for her own behavior. Insults build up inside as thoughts are allowed to invade the mind like, "Nobody could have it that much together—you can see she needs to lose 10 pounds, there is evidently no discipline in her life." Then the *cement* of the influence of others is added. You are committed to behave according to the words of your mouth in criticism. You find it difficult to change and your attitude demands that you ask forgiveness of God, and appropriate His power to change your attitude.

The thing that troubled me so much as I had to face the criticism of others is that I sensed the critical spirit being formed in me. Leaders are particularly open to this problem because they take risks that tend to draw criticism. God has forgiven and is continuing to cleanse, and I thank and praise Him for this provision for my sin.

Ralph Carmichael told my husband that he has discovered a confirmation that God was doing a work in his life. He is a musician, publisher, composer, arranger, and director. Hundreds of pieces of music cross his desk annually, many sent by aspiring composers. He says, "It was a moment of deep joy when I realized that I was as happy about another musician's success as my own!"

### The Builder

Now, back to the Word for a look at those steps to being a *constructive* influence. There are several lists in the Scripture of the qualities of one who builds up, but 2 Peter 1:5-8,10 presents a ladder toward the character of Christ within us.

"But to obtain these gifts [his character] you need more than faith; you must also work hard to be good, and even that is not enough. For then you must learn to know God better and discover what he wants you to do. Next, learn to put aside your own desires so that you will become patient and godly, gladly letting God have his way with you. This will make possible the next step, which is for you to enjoy the other people and to like them, and finally you will grow to love them deeply. The more you go on in this way, the more you will grow strong spiritually and become fruitful and useful to our Lord Jesus Christ. . . . So, dear brothers, *work hard* to prove that you really are among those God has called and chosen" (*TLB*, italics added).

Bottom step is *Faith*. If your faith has brought you through to a knowledge of Jesus Christ as your Saviour where you can claim His promises, then add to your faith step 2:

*Goodness*. Fix your thoughts and mind on being good. Ethel Barrett has written a book entitled *Don't Look Now—But Your Personality Is Showing*, She struggled with goodness and humility in this situation:

"A young woman came to me without a job and without a Saviour and very, very broke, materially and spiritually. I introduced her to Christ, gave her some clothes and a wee bit of money, and by some miracle I had a contact that landed her a job as a clerk in a department store. I blessed her and prayed with her and sent her on the way. And I felt so noble I could hardly stand it.

"Two years later she phoned me. She's done well, and was now a buyer of women's clothing in another city. She was just passing through. Did I want to have lunch? I did. I could hardly wait to hear her outpourings of gratitude and to give her some more encouragement, peppered with my wisdom and counsel.

"The jolt came when I met her in a downtown restaurant. She had more money on her back in one outfit than I could afford to spend in a year. . . . She pulled off her kid gloves. I pulled off my cotton gloves. She looked at me, wide-eyed and said, 'Hasn't the Lord been wonderful?'

"Full-blown, into my mind it came. All at once, and more quickly than it can be told. 'What do you mean, the Lord? Me and the Lord. I gave you money. . . .'

"I gave that to the Lord at once in the same flash with which it had come to me, and I am more ashamed of it than of many more heinous crimes I have committed. Telling about it takes a paragraph; actually it was only a twinge. But the implications of that twinge are horrendous!"[5]

Let us swiftly release anything that is not good, as we add goodness to our faith.

Step 6 is *Knowledge*. Hosea 6:3 says: "Let us acknowledge the Lord; let us press on to acknowledge him."

"Then, *Patience* and *Perseverence*. Sticktuitiveness. You be the builder who is not too quick to turn over the job to someone else. Patiently learn to build right there on your part of the wall, and you will move on up the ladder to *Godliness*. Godliness will include the development of *holy habits*—consistent church involvement, quiet times with the Lord, speaking the truth in love to everyone might be some of these.

Step 7 is *Kindness*. In *The Living Bible* it is a phrase: "to enjoy other people." My mother-in-love exuded kindness. A woman of great spiritual strength and influence, she plainly enjoyed people. Perhaps the most important reason I trusted her so much was the fact that she spoke *kindly* of everyone. After my husband and I had been married just a couple of years, she presented me with a beautiful afghan she had thoughtfully crocheted during many long hours of her and Dad's traveling ministry. A kindness that was backed up with the knowledge that I was not being "run down," destroyed by any word of hers "behind the wall." Because I had never heard her criticize another, there was no reason to even think that she would speak unkindly of me. A character quality to be pursued, don't you think?

Step 8 is *Love*—1 Corinthians 13 love. Build in others' lives with love in the same proportion Christ has loved you!

Never let it be said that we have discouraged others from leadership because of criticism of those who are now leading. Who would want to be in that spot—to receive, even attract criticism? A wise woman builds, says a wise man in Proverbs 14.

> All have a share in the beauty, all have a part in
>         the plan.
> What does it matter what duty falls to the lot of
>         a man?
> Someone has blended the plaster; someone
>         has carried the stone;
> Neither the man nor the Master ever has
>         builded alone;
> Make a roof for the weather, building a house
>         for the King;
> Only by working together have men accom-
>         plished a thing.[6]

## Notes

1. Amy Carmichael, *If* (Fort Washington, PA: Christian Literature Crusade, 1966).
2. Daisy Hepburn, *Why Doesn't Somebody Do Something?* (Wheaton, IL: Victor Books, 1980), p. 87.
3. John Stott, *Guard the Gospel* (Downers Grove, IL: Inter-Varsity Press, 1973), pp. 67, 68.
4. Author unknown
5. Ethel Barrett, *Don't Look Now—But Your Personality Is Showing* (Ventura, CA: Regal Books, 1968), p. 44.
6. Author unknown.

\* For your sample write: Daisy Hepburn, c/o Regal Books, Box 3875, Ventura, CA 93006.

# Eight

# The Vessel

"In a large house there are articles not only of gold and silver, but also of wood and clay; some are for noble purposes and some for ignoble. If a man cleanses himself from the latter, he will be an instrument for noble purposes, made holy, useful to the Master and prepared to do any good work." (2 Tim. 2:20,21).

Next week, everyone bring a vessel and you will be surprised what we will do with it!" The 40 children in front of me had a gleam in their eyes, as they contemplated our next meeting's possibilities.

Then Bobby piped up, "What is a vessel anyway, Daisy?"

"Anything that can hold something, I guess, Bobby. So bring something you think might be a vessel, and we will see if it works. Use your imagination and look all around the grounds, or ask your cottage mother."

David and I were at the children's home. Of the 130 children on the grounds of the 700-acre site in the rolling hills of northern California, I had the happy opportunity to lead almost half of them in the Sunday evening service. I was trying to teach the boys and girls about how God can use each of us, and what a privilege it is to be a vessel for Him.

Next Sunday arrived, and so did the kids—and the vessels—

Rusty tin cans, empty pop bottles, chipped cups, flower pots—every size and shape imaginable. We lined them all up on the mantel of the fireplace. My idea was to put a sweet potato into each of them, fill them with water and let the kids observe and enjoy the quickly growing vines.

The water flowed—the kids decided they would like to do it themselves. The pitchers were filled in the rest rooms and poured into the vessels. WHOOPS! We discovered vessels that were not usable. The water flowed down over the bricks and into the fireplace and all over the floor.

We managed to salvage a couple of dozen that were watertight, and I deposited a many-eyed sweet potato into each one. The kids were watching to see if the potatoes would sprout on the spot. We waited until the next week—and the next. I could not decide what the problem was, why the leaves had not emerged from the vessels.

We found out! We arrived for our Sunday evening class and the smell in the room was overpowering! The potatoes were blobs of rotten stuff, and we were crushed. The lesson was a bit less than effective as far as the children were concerned, but I learned a great deal.

The condition of the *vessel* is of utmost importance. The vessel must be *clean*. All the rust and residue in the variety of vessels the children had offered worked to rot the contents. The container has a greater influence on the contents than we realized.

Second Timothy 2 gives us our sixth portrait of God's servant-leader. The vessel is the only inanimate figure in this chapter. As with the other portraits we will consider first some insights for our lives as individual women, then the practical application for our service—that is, ways to have a ministry of prayer.

### Holy Purpose

If you were to glance in your concordance, you would see how often references are made to clay, the potter, vessels, and usefulness. Five kinds of vessels are described from which we will illustrate some uses that God might have in mind for each of us.

1. *Earthen vessels.* Tucked into the many, many word pictures of Paul's letters to the Corinthians is this verse, "This priceless treasure we hold, so to speak, in a common earthenware jar—to show that the splendid power of it belongs to God and not to us" (2 Cor. 4:7, *Phillips*).

Have you ever seen a potter at work? He picks up the lump of clay and begins to shape it to his liking. He presses and pokes and pulls and spins it on his wheel. The product reflects the skill of the potter. After the clay is dry, the potter fires the vessel. Vessels made by potters in Bible days which were fired once were used for storing grain or other dry foods. A water jug—or vessel of honor—must be fired again before it can be used, and it must be glazed.

A clay flower pot is good for growing plants, but its use is limited because it is porous. As with every kind of vessel, it has no control over how it is used; and its value is determined by what it contains.

"When a craftsman makes anything he doesn't expect it to turn around and say, 'Why did you make me like this?' The potter, for instance, is always assumed to have complete control over the clay, making with one part of the lump a lovely vase, and with another a pipe for sewage. Can we not assume that God has the same control over human clay?" (Rom. 9:21, *Phillips*).

When we submit to the wooing power of the Lord

and receive Jesus by faith, we become earthen vessels. We have been formed to contain a priceless treasure— the power of God and the message of the love of Jesus. And He will use us, though we have been "newly formed."

The Master stood in His garden among the lil-
    ies fair,
Which His own hand had planted and trained
    with tend'rest care.

He looked at their snowy blossoms and
    marked with observant eye
That His flowers were sadly drooping for their
    leaves were parched and dry.

"My lilies need to be watered," the Heavenly
    Master said;
"Wherein shall I draw it for them, and raise
    each drooping head?"

Close to His feet on the pathway, empty and
    frail and small,
An earthen vessel was lying, which seemed of
    no use at all.

But the Master saw, and raised it from the dust
    in which it lay,
And smiled as He gently whispered; "This shall
    do my work today.

"It is but an earthen vessel, but it lay so close to
    me;
It is small, but it is empty, and that is all it needs
    to be."

So to the fountain He took it, and filled it to the
    brim;

How glad was the earthen vessel to be of some
use to Him!

He poured forth the living water over His lilies
fair,
Until the vessel was empty, and again He filled
it there.

He watered the drooping lilies until they
revived again,
And the Master saw with pleasure, that His
labor was not in vain.

His own hand had drawn the water which
refreshed the thirsty flowers
But He used the earthen vessel to convey the
living showers.

And to itself it whispered, as He laid it aside
once more.
"Still will I lie in His pathway, Just where I did
before.

Close would I be to the Master and empty
would I remain.
Some day He may use me to water His flowers
again."[1]

But there is more for the woman who is willing to be
further shaped, and "fired" for further service.

2. *Vessels of honor and dishonor.* I have been told
that the waterjug occupied a very obvious position in
front of every rural Palestinian home. Near the front
doorstep stood the vessel of honor, and at the opposite
side the vessel of dishonor was located. Fresh water was
daily brought from the well in the village and the vessel of
honor was filled. All waste was collected in the vessel of

dishonor.

Second Timothy 2:20 describes these vessels. The vessel of honor must be kept scrupulously clean. It is used only for fresh water and is even a sign of hospitality. Besides the family, travelers are refreshed from this jug. This water is also used for cleansing.

How do the vessels of honor and dishonor differ from the earthen vessel? They have been to the fire the second time. There is a glaze that not only keeps the clay from absorbing the water, but also acts as a thermal agent. Paul says of the vessel of honor, "If a man keeps himself clean from the contaminations of evil he will be a vessel used for honorable purpose, clean and serviceable for the use of the master of the household" (2 Tim. 2:21, *Phillips*).

The vessel of dishonor has also been fired twice, but it is used for refuse. It often looks the same on the outside but all that is poured into it is dirty or left over. Cleanliness is unimportant to this vessel.

"Whatever He says to you, do it!" The mother of Jesus at the festive wedding in Cana gave that direction to the servants. It must have been an orthodox home as well as a rather wealthy one, for there were six waterpots standing there, each holding 20 to 30 gallons. Those were VESSELS! Jesus used these vessels of honor to reveal His power and begin His public ministry.

Imagine having the submission to obey to the extent that you were willing to fill the waterpots to the tune of 180 gallons!

A miracle was performed and the contents of the vessels were transformed. (See John 2:1-11.)

That is what I want to have happen in my life.

Again we see that the image is flexible. It is apparent that we *can* be responsible for the contents of this vessel—although it is an inanimate object—in order that the lesson the Scripture teaches can be applied.

For example, we can CHOOSE to take another step

in usability.

3. *Chosen vessels.* These vessels have gone through
the fire several times. There are often special markings
and designs on the finish of these jars or vases. If the potter wants to make a gift to you, he may say, "Here is my
choice for you. Take this one; it will never put me to
shame. Take this vessel to your home—it reflects the skill
of the maker. It is a *chosen vessel.*"

Do you know a chosen vessel? These are those who
have been made stronger because of the fire. They gleam
and shine with the design of God in their lives. It is as if
they have been stamped with the mark of the Maker.

Lots of chosen vessels are prayer partners of mine.

Lucille Erickson is one of my special friends. Just a
few years my senior, she is less than five feet tall and
weighs about half of what I do. Just under a year ago her
eye had to be removed. Did that stop her? Not for a minute—well, maybe for a minute or two. But she has been
to the fire more often than most of us. Because of the
many firings, she is stronger and more useful. Her wit and
determination are beyond my comprehension. Dragging
herself out of bed she arranges parties for "old folks,"
most of whom are more able than she is. Cutting up old
greeting cards and cleverly reassembling them doesn't
sound like a very high level activity for Jesus' sake. When
the mailman leaves one for me with a love note inside,
this old vessel of mine quivers with the knowledge that I
have been remembered and prayed for.

When the Indian church in Minneapolis burned to the
ground last year, who spearheaded a relief operation?
You're right, Lucille!

If it is possible to have a ministry through needlework
and note writing, then Lucille has found it. She is clean,
filled and available for miracles to be worked in her. A
chosen vessel, indeed.

Lucille and I share a penchant for Ziggy, the loser.
Lucy clipped a particularly appropriate cartoon and sent

it to me. Ziggy is pictured flat on his back, puffing and panting and saying, "My energy level reached its peak two years ago—but I think I slept through it!"

She must depend deeply on the filling of the Lord in her life for physical as well as spiritual power.

Dr. Harold Fickett shared the following pattern for how we can respond to the challenge of Ephesians 5:18 to be filled with the Spirit.

*Aspire* to be controlled by the Spirit of God—Romans 8:5 and 8:30.

*Acknowledge* your sin and receive cleansing—Psalm 66:18.

*Abandon* yourself to His purposes for you—Romans 9:23,24.

*Ask* the Holy Spirit to fill you—James 4:2.

*Accept* by faith the fact of His filling—Colossians 2:6.[2]

4. *Broken vessels.* David cried out in Psalm 31:12, "I have become like broken pottery." He felt useless and cast aside. Good news! There is a use for even broken vessels.

In homes in Bible times these pieces of broken vessels, called sherds, were used to carry live coals. Sherds carried warmth, perhaps from a neighbor's fire, to rekindle a spark. Sherds are broken, ill-shaped and have nothing in themselves to be proud of—but they carry live coals!

In many of our churches there are those women whose lives have been broken or damaged either with or without any action or decision on their own parts. Often they feel that they can never be used again. How good it is to bask in the restorative grace of God. If you are that person, or have the opportunity to minister to some "broken vessels," take heart! God isn't finished with you yet—and He delights in using broken things. It is often our own judgmental attitudes that keep those whose lives have been broken from enjoying a new usefulness.

But don't you be a breaker! Lives—as vessels—are

fragile, and we need to take care to treat each other carefully.

5. *Vessels of service.* When God instructed Moses to build the Tabernacle He gave definite commands about the furnishings and the vessels to be used in the holy place. They were to be set apart, never used for anything else, and they were to be sanctified for holy purposes.

This is the highest form of usefulness for a vessel. Set apart, sanctified for service. And to think we can by faith be prepared for this:

"Take the anointing oil and anoint the tabernacle and everything in it; consecrate it and all its furnishings, and it will be holy. Then anoint the altar of burnt offering and all its utensils; consecrate the altar, and it will be most holy. Anoint the basin and its stand and consecrate them" (Exod. 40:9-11).

Oil in the Scriptures is always a type of the Holy Spirit. How were the vessels used for special service to be made holy? By anointing with oil. They were to be kept for high and holy services. Never to be used for common tasks.

Pompous King Belshazzar gave a great banquet for a thousand of his nobles. While drinking his wine, he gave orders to have golden goblets brought to the banquet. They were the sanctified goblets from the Temple in Jerusalem. They were valuable to captive Israelites beyond any understanding of the drunken king of Babylon or his cohorts.

Daniel was called in to interpret Belshazzar's vision of the writing on the wall. With great courage and supernatural power, Daniel dared to tell the king that God had judged him, and part of that judgment was because he had desecrated the vessels from the Temple.

Vessels of service are not to be used for common things.

"If you stay away from sin you will be like one of these dishes made of purest gold—the very best in the house—so that Christ himself can use you for his highest purposes" (2 Tim. 2:21, *TLB*).

You and I can choose to be set apart for service. May nothing less be satisfactory. If God has chosen you for His service, then make sure that your life is kept clean. Never allow Satan to dupe you into thinking you can take part in common things. Be a vessel for service in the house of the Lord.

> Lord, how can I a chosen vessel be, to bear
>     Thy name to others far and near—
> That precious message carried, Lord, by me,
>     An earthen vessel, frail and full of fear?
> Lord, what if this weak vessel e'er should
>     break,
> Leaving someone without a taste of Thee?
>
> "I know," said He, "that thou art frail to bear
>     the message I have put within thy soul;
> But nothing that is handled with great care is
>     broken, though it be a fragile bowl.
> I chose thee not for any strength of thine;
> But thou art in My hand, O child of mine."[3]

### Ministry in Prayer

Set apart for special service. One of the highest and holiest services we can give is that of prayer. You can have a ministry in prayer.

My suggestion is that you first examine your own prayer life. Are you on intimate speaking terms with your Father in heaven?

Some wonderful books on prayer have been written and excellent helps provided. A simple prayer pattern is probably not new or unfamiliar to you, but I give it again because it might well be the basis for your own life as well as for an intercessory ministry.

*Prayer Pattern*. The acts of prayer might include these

four areas.

A—Adoration or worship; Psalm 34:1—Exalt His name.

C—Confession; Psalm 66:18—If I regard iniquity in my heart, the Lord will not hear me.

T—Thanksgiving; Psalm 92:1—It is a good thing to give thanks unto the Lord!

S—Supplication; Philippians 4:6—By prayer and supplication . . . let your requests be made known unto God.

As you go to the Lord in prayer, go worshipfully. Consider spending a few moments simply acknowledging God for who He is. Worship Him in the beauty of the Scripture. Read back to your Father the words of Psalm 103 which is a list of all He can be to you.

Include a time of confession in your personal prayer. Confess first all known sin. The Holy Spirit is faithful to let us know those areas of need when we pray, "Search me, O God, and know my heart; test me and know my anxious thoughts. See if there is any offensive way in me, and lead me in the way everlasting" (Ps. 139:23,24).

Do not carry guilt. God intends that we keep short accounts with Him. Realize that just as quickly as you confess your sin, forgiveness is yours. Why are we slow to appropriate His grace in forgiveness? Be a vessel who knows victory in prayer because you have been both willing and able to release your guilt to your Saviour who has already paid for it!

My friend was sharing some frustration with me about a certain loved one of hers—her son. She said that she has always taught her children that they should not partake in the elements of the communion table if they were not up-to-the-minute with the Lord. So, friend son became careless and declined to take the elements. Finally this chosen vessel friend of mine confronted her son with the good news that forgiveness was instantaneous—just as soon as we confess and express a desire for that forgiveness we are forgiven. Sin is not a condition you have to live with; you can know freedom from guilt right now. Sometimes it is more comfortable to co-exist with a few faults than to assume the responsibility that freedom and holy living afford.

Now, thank the Lord in everything. Be careful not to thank God for everything—there is so much sin and sorrow around us that He is not responsible for. But thank Him for His faithfulness in the midst of the trial, and for His promises for the future. Thank Him for His peace in the storm. Thank Him for all those conveniences that more than meet your need for more time.

As you come to the Lord with your requests, it is a good idea to have a list of those needs and persons for which you are responsible to pray. A point of frustration in our praying, particularly for leaders who want to pray for those with whom they serve and those whom they lead, is the impossibility of praying for everyone every day. Divide the list and pray for just a portion of those needs each day. Missionaries, church members, neighbors, leaders of our nation and communities need our prayers. Better to pray for fewer each day and to pray in depth.

*Prayer participation.* Get involved in praying with others. Here are some guidelines for forming a prayer chain, as suggested by Evelyn Christianson's United Prayer Ministries in Minneapolis.[4]

HOW DO YOU START? Get together with one or two other mature pray-ers and seek God's will. His will may be for you to pray together for a while before enlarging the group. If you're starting a church prayer group or chain, make sure you have the blessing of your pastor and that he agrees to help if you need guidance. (If he doesn't agree, go back and pray for God's timing.)

HOW MANY MEMBERS? Keep your group or chain small. There is more chance of each person participating this way. If it grows large, break into small groups or chains.

WHAT ABOUT RULES? Have specific rules and leaders who are mature Christians and can enforce them.

a. Start at a specific time and end on time (1 Cor. 14:40).

b. Keep a watch on confidences shared (Ps. 141:3).

c. Emphasize the need for private, daily prayer (John 15:7).

d. Live cleansed lives (1 John 1:9).

e. Decide what time and how many requests should go through the chain each day. Too many will exhaust pray-ers.

f. Pray requests, not answers.

g. Keep a list of your requests and answers for encouragement.

h. Meet together for times of sharing and getting acquainted.

i. Be honest! When problems arise, or even if you see one coming, talk to your leader about it. Don't let bitterness begin (Heb. 12:15).

j. Be sure to spend time praising—even if you don't see the answers to your prayers at the time (Ps. 92:1,2).

k. Be sure to put on the full armor of God! (Eph. 6:11-18).

*Pray for Others*. Get involved in intercession. A couple of weeks ago, Rosella, one of my most faithful prayer partners, wrote me one more of her encouraging notes and enclosed the following article. She asked me how I would like to be prayed for according to this Scripture. I responded quickly with a resounding yes. It is an article by Sarah Gudschinsky, a longtime missionary with the Wycliffe Bible Translators.

"In Colossians 1:9-13—'For this cause we also, since the day we heard it, do not cease to pray for you, and to desire that ye might be filled with the knowledge of his will in all wisdom and spiritual understanding; that ye might walk worthy of the Lord unto all pleasing, being fruitful in every good work, and increasing in the knowledge of God; strengthened with all might, according to his glorious power, unto all patience and longsuffering with joyfulness; giving thanks unto the Father, which hath made us meet to be partakers of the inheritance of the saints in light: who hath delivered us from the power of darkness, and hath translated us into the kingdom of his dear Son . . .'

"Lord, bless Charles . . . and bless the Gregersons, and bless Marge, and bless . . .

"This is the tenth of June, and custom demands that I pray for my fellow workers listed on 'Day 10' of the prayer directory. I don't know very many of these people personally, and I don't have any news, so my prayer is dry and hurried and impersonal—bless the Grubers, and bless . . . wait a minute!

"The next name on the list is my own. And I wonder with shock and horror if others today are praying ' . . . and bless Sarah and bless Shirley . . . and . . .' not really praying for *me* at all.

"The apostle Paul lived in a time of poor communication and lack of news. He carried a heavy prayer burden for churches and individuals. Yet I have no impression that his prayer was hurried or dry. It occurs to me that if I use Scripture as a base for my prayer, it may become more meaningful—more like the prayer I need from others.

"I think I'll try it with Colossians 1.

"Lord, fill Charles with a knowledge of Thy will. May he have Thy point of view in all things. Keep him from decisions made for self-advantage or according to the perverted standards of this world.

"Give him wisdom and spiritual understanding. Deliver him from a dependence on the dishonesty and craftiness of man's wisdom, from conceit and pride.

Grant to him the wisdom which is from above—pure, teachable, humble.

"Grant that he might bring credit to Thy name and please Thee in all things.
Enable him for this not only in his praying and witnessing, but also in the drudgeries of daily living. May small maintenance jobs, errands run, meals eaten, the way he dresses and all else please Thee.

"Make him fruitful in good works.
Keep him from any self-centeredness or even work-centeredness that would keep him from acts of kindness and goodness and generosity.

"Increase his knowledge of Thee.
May he see Thee clearly in Thy Word, may he fellowship with Thee in prayer and meditation, may he be so filled with the Spirit of holiness that he may see Thee in truth.

"Strengthen him with all Thy glorious power—the power that raised Christ from the dead.
Take his weakness and inability that it might be lost in the ocean depths of Thine own omnipotence.

"Teach him patience and long-suffering.
Make him patient with the shortcomings and irritating habits of his co-workers, in all the daily annoyance and friction. Make him patient in the multitude of interruptions to the problem that he has laid out. Give him long-suffering in the unreasonable upsets and delays which slow the work. And grant to him patience with himself, with his own faults and weakness.

"Fill his heart with overflowing joy.
May he see Thy overruling love and mercy in every circumstance. May he rejoice in opportunities to show forth the patience and meekness that come from Thee.

"Praise be unto Thee, O Lord our God,
that Thou hast made Charles to be fit to be a partaker of the inheritance of the saints of light. I thank Thee for Thy mercy and transforming power in his life.

"I thank Thee for calling him out of the domain of

darkness and into the kingdom of Thy dear Son. I pray that Thou wouldst make the deliverance from darkness and sin a practical reality in his daily life. Bring him quickly to conviction and repentance when he falls into sin.

"And may all glory be unto Jesus our Lord and Saviour whose is the preeminence in all things. Amen."[5]

### Creative Praying

If you are reading this while alone, why not take this moment to go and fill your vessel with some hot coffee or tea, and then think creatively with me about some ways to have a prayer ministry. All set? Here goes with 7 ideas:

1. *Pray through your Christmas cards!* My dear mother and daddy give and receive hundreds of Christmas cards each year. At their retirement they decided to expand their prayer ministry. As November and December arrive each year, so do the cards. They are collected in a large, attractive basket. At the first of the new year, two cards are drawn daily and the senders are prayed for in their morning devotions. Then Mom writes a postcard to those prayed for with a note of encouragement. The cards are special ones that say "We have prayed for you today" and are available through Good News Publishers, 9825 W. Roosevelt Road, Westchester, Illinois, 60153. Attractive prayer postcards are also available through The American Tract Society, P.O. Box 402008, Garland, Texas, 75040.

2. *Prayer partners.* Four years ago I realized through a friend's suggestion that my own ministry would be enriched through the sharing of concerns with prayer partners. I wrote a note to 31 women friends, mostly from our home church, and invited them to become a partner in believing prayer with me one day each month. Each of them said yes. I made a list and assigned each of them one day and committed myself to pray for each lady on her day. About once a quarter I send a letter to

each of my—now 62—prayer partners and give them my schedule, as well as share some of the answers received. Many of them write to me to let me know how to pray specifically for them. How the Lord has blessed us all. If each reader were to set up her own network, just think about the prayer support God's women across the land would supply for His work!

3. *Day Starters*. This is an idea the Lord gave to encourage both new Christians as well as help those "older" ones to the discipline of beginning the day with the Lord.

    a. Phone a partner at an agreed upon time— same time each day 'till further notice. Let her call you the second week.

    b. Set oven timer for three minutes.

    c. First minute will be to share a prayer request or a note of praise.

    d. Second minute is to read a five-or-six verse portion of Scripture. It is good to read through a book of the Bible together.

    e. Either one or both of you pray for the last minute.

    Hang up as the bell rings!

At the end of the first month, try it again with either the same partner or another. Simply enjoy the encouragement and discipline!

4. *Key 16*. There are 16 elected government officials who have a direct impact on the life of you and your family. The Scripture teaches that we are to pray for those in authority. One way of doing that is to make a list of the names of those 16 elected officials and make it a special prayer list. It might take some research on your part to come up with them, but perhaps it is time that you get acquainted with those whose decisions affect you and yours.

U. S. Government Five—President
                             Vice-President

                    Senator
                    Senator
                    Congressman
State Government Five—Governor
                    Lt. Governor
                    Attorney General
                    State Senator
                    Assemblyman
Local Government Six—Mayor
                    City Councilman
                    City Attorney
                    School Board Member
                    County Supervisor
                    Sheriff

Why not, at least occasionally, write a letter to these people to indicate that you are praying for them. It just might make their day!

5. *Make a devotional booklet*. Ask your prayer partners or members of your prayer group or circle to write a prayer or psalm or short meditation. They could be typed and instant-printed or copied attractively. Then each contributor could use her copy of the composite booklet as her prayer guide for Advent or Lent or some special period of time. The same idea could be used for family devotions. Several families could prepare their own prayers and then assemble a booklet.

6. *Directed Prayer*. This is an idea for leading prayer in larger groups. This method of leading prayer seems to accomplish two special things: (1) it allows for maximum participation without any one person or persuasion to monopolize the entire prayer time; (2) the leader both opens and closes the prayer time, so there is a control.

The leader begins by giving simple instructions: "We are going to pray together, in small groups. Make a group of four or five. (If your people are seated around tables make certain that the group will be able to hear one another, or divide your groups again. If they are seated in rows, invite every other row to turn around so that they can pray in circles rather than rows.)

"We are going to pray together for several subjects. I will give you the topic and then will ask one or two of you in each group to pray briefly—just a sentence or two—for that subject, then I will give the next topic.

"After a few minutes of prayer I will conclude with prayer."

Depending on the size and purpose of your gathering, you might want to recruit a prayer hostess for each table or location. Also you might want to have prayer lists already available for prayer leaders, or even for all in attendance. Consider having each small group spend two or three minutes getting acquainted and compiling their own prayer list and allow those needs to be prayed for during the last few minutes of your prayer time before you conclude.

Exchanging name tags within those groups for further prayer partnerships is another way of confirming the time spent together.

7. *Put it in a basket!* This idea was born out of necessity. A special outreach women's meeting—Spice of Life—was flourishing. However, the prayer time was becoming a drag! Many of the women attending were not accustomed to either lengthy or public prayer. Some of the leaders were feeling that prayer was a necessary part of the meeting, but how to control it. The ladies coming had special needs—including the need to be noticed and affirmed (is there any among us who do not have that need!). Listen a minute to what was happening:

"Good morning, ladies. We are glad to have a few minutes to spend in prayer together. Are there any requests today?

"My nephew has a broken ankle in Fort Worth. My sister, his mother, has had to leave work to take care of him, and her vacation time is already spent. If her husband would help her more she would not have to take valuable time off work to keep her home together. Will you pray that my sister and brother-in-law work this out and that my nephew will heal so that he can get back to his paper route, and . . . and . . . ad infinitum.

"All right, we will pray for that. Did you all remember those names? Are there others?"

"My sister-in-law in Kansas City . . ."

"Our dog is lost—son—husband—" "The screen door—neighbors' dissension—and on and on."

You have been in meetings like this one, haven't you? The prayer time was taking over! And the ladies were uncomfortable not only with the involved and often irrelevant prayer requests, but with the necessary time spent in praying for each one.

Here is how the problem was wonderfully solved:

a. Small attractive baskets were already on the tables for offering, along with welcome packets. Several slips of paper were included.

b. The leader suggested that anyone with a special prayer request write it on one of the slips of paper. (She can sign it if she likes and include her phone number if she would like someone to call her either for encouragement or for prayer over the telephone.)

c. In a few minutes the prayer request slips were collected in a basket, and prayer was offered for them generally.

d. Those who were willing to pray raised their hands and the basket was passed and they each drew a slip to take home for the week.

It works!

"This is the word that came to Jeremiah from the Lord, 'Go down to the potter's house, and there I will give you my message.' So I went down to the potter's house, and I saw him working at the wheel. But the pot he was shaping from the clay was marred in his hands; so the potter formed it into another pot, shaping it as seemed best to him. Then the word of the Lord came to me: 'O house of Israel, can I not do with you as this potter does?' declares the Lord. 'Like clay in the hand of the potter, so are you in my hand' " (Jer. 18:1-6).

> Have thine own way, Lord! Have Thine own
> way!
> Thou are the Potter, I am the clay.
> Mold me and make me after Thy will
> While I am waiting, yielded and still.

> Have Thine own way, Lord! Have Thine own
> way!
> Hold o'er my being absolute sway
> Fill with Thy Spirit 'til all shall see
> Christ only, always living in me![6]

   Be a vessel whose abilities are simply . . . AVAIL-ability, USE-abilty, ADAPT-ability, RESPONS-ability and you will be a vessel meet for the Master's use.

**Notes**
1. Author unknown
2. From a sermon by Harold L. Fickett, Jr.
3. Author unknown
4. Adapted from United Prayer Ministries.
5. Sarah Gudschinsky, from a tract published by Wycliffe Bible Translators.
6. Adalaide A. Pollard, "Have Thine Own Way, Lord."

## Nine

# The Servant

"And the Lord's servant must not quarrel; instead, he must be kind to everyone, able to teach, not resentful" (2 Tim. 2:24).

"It's a great summer job, Daisy. Besides, where else can you make that kind of money and still go to the beach every day?"

A college friend talked me into a summer job at a large hotel on the Atlantic Coast, waiting on tables. Of course, there were a few details she neglected to include, like the fact that the base salary would just about cover a summer's beach pass and a hot dog or two on the board-walk after hours occasionally. One other, the "servants' quarters" in that hotel were five flights *up*—and I shared my room right under the hot, tin roof, with 15 or 20 other waitresses.

The design was that the low salary was to encourage you to do your job so well, and to be so alert and avail-able, that you could retire early on your tips. That part of it has always been a problem for me—is the customer then responsible for the salary of the servant, or is the employer? Ah well, the summer flew by, and with all our complaining we returned to college as brown and chubby as could be.

Now when we are enjoying pie and coffee in a nearby restaurant, we sometimes evaluate the service and discuss the amount of the tip. My husband forgets how many times he has given me this morsel of information, "Do you know what tip really means?" Playing dumb, I bite and he recites, "To Insure Promptness, that's what it means!"

Then we proceed to dig into our pockets and come up with what we think our waitress's promptness deserves. A silly game, and yet we are part of a society that seems to insure rewards for service.

God has His own system and invites us to live by this system with a fresh newness in all we do and think.

Tips help, to be sure, but God is interested in a glad spirit, willing hands, and a servant heart.

Remember right at the beginning: The Scripture's pattern for leadership is in becoming a servant of the Living God!

> Life can never be dull again
> When once you've thrown the window open
> wide
> And seen the great world that lies outside—
> And said to yourself this wondrous thing:
> "I'm wanted for the service of the King!"[1]

The picture of a bond servant occurs often in Scripture. A slave served his master out of obligation. Sometimes the master would choose to free the slave. Then it was up to the slave to decide whether or not he wanted to continue to serve his master. If he chose to do so, he became a bond servant and wore a mark that indicated his status.

Whom do you serve?

Why do you serve?

A finely dressed nobleman passed the slave auction block and heard the auctioneer shouting the merits of the strong, robust, dejected slave being sold. The man began to bid, higher and higher, and to the surprise of the onlookers, soon found himself the owner of the other man, the slave.

As he was summoned to take ownership, he paid for his purchase and then proceeded to loose the bonds and said with pity, "Take off the chains; I have bought you to free you! Go!"

The slave threw himself at the master's feet and cried out, "Please let me serve you for the rest of my life. Let me be your slave, by love!"

Is this verse, learned by many of us in childhood, too simplistic for the complicated ministries in our lives: "Serve one another in love" (Gal. 5:13)? Let's hope not!

It is inconvenient to be a servant—often uncomfortable.

Can you see how dealing gracefully with *interruptions* requires a servant heart?

Can you see how to find purpose and meaning in *routine* requires a servant heart?

Can you see how assuming the risky role of *leadership* requires a servant heart?

But there is so little in our present worldly society that encourages the attitude of willing service to others. What has conditioned you in your life to be willing to serve?

Paul had a Damascus-Road-flash of lightning call to service. But Martha served because she was the only one who would do it. Lots of our service is done simply because no one else will. Martha had difficulty handling interruptions. As a matter of fact, she got right riled up about them. Her leadership in that home was a problem to her; there were other things maybe she would like to have done. When things get too bad, she did what we had all better do, she went right to the Saviour with her complaints.

What a relationship to enjoy with Jesus. When bothered about much serving and the lack of support from my "sisters" I will go to Jesus and risk a rebuke from Him—or risk a change in my own attitude.

Apparently she learned a lesson about serving, because there she is again, waiting on tables in John 12 at a banquet in Jesus' honor. Mary anointed Jesus' feet, doing what she could, and received the loving approval of her Lord. Martha's service was another sort of sacrifice.

> Take my life, and let it be
> Consecrated, Lord, to Thee;
> ......................................................
>
> Take my moments and my days,
> Let them flow in ceaseless praise.[2]

Let's look at the servant's characteristics.

*A servant is willing to serve!* A true love slave serves with gladness. When Isaiah was touched by God with the vision of live coals cleansing and sanctifying him and then was challenged to service and witness, his response was clear, "Here am I. Send me!" (Isa. 6:8).

An executive for a major airline said, "Our greatest problem is finding men and women who are willing to serve. Everyone wants to lead. No one wants to serve."

Since serving is the scriptural way—and if we want to serve gladly, not under protest—let's go one more time to the altar for another touch of the live coal.

Both the title and the contents of a current book trouble me.

*Our Struggle to Serve* is a collection of experiences of several gifted Christian women as they have struggled with the finding of their place in the ministry of Jesus Christ. Is it a struggle to serve Christ, or is the struggle to submit to the servant's role? Women, even in the Body of

Christ and in His established church, are being bombarded with pressures to assert their rights. Some struggle to be in church leadership in congregations and denominations that are not designed for this. There is so much work to be done, so much serving; please, ladies, let's get on with it. A love slave gives up his rights in order to fulfill his responsibilities.

*A servant is unselfish.* Another paradox in serving is found in the Golden Rule. You do for others what you wish others would do for you. When you are tired or discouraged or tempted to self-pity in service, pick yourself up, dust yourself off, and learn to live by Jesus' ethic. What do you need from others? Loyalty? Give yourself loyally to Christ and those around you as never before! Do you need encouragement? (Wow, do I need encouragement!) Then sit yourself down and write at least three notes to encourage someone else. Do you need some attention or affirmation? Begin to *think* like Christ. Do what Jesus would do and phone someone who is seldom recognized.

As I write these words I can look up at the wall of this room and, among other significant signs, mottoes and photos, is this one, specially framed: "Ask not what your mother can do for you, ask what you can do for your mother."

Most of our kids have no idea about the Golden Rule at home, do they? Will someone tell them about how much we need affirmation and service, especially service behind our own front door?

Well, if Erma Bombeck isn't all that successful in getting her kids to work, perhaps I should take heart. She remembers those days when it was all she could do to get the five basic sentences out of her mouth, much less worry about their learning to work—

1. Close the door.
2. Don't talk with food in your mouth.
3. Check out the clothes hamper.

4. I saw you playing with the dog so go wash your hands.

5. You should have gone before you left home.

Back to the servant—

A servant is obedient. "Now the most important thing about a servant is that he does just what his master tells him to" (1 Cor. 4:2, *TLB*).

A servant has a submissive spirit. "And all of you serve each other with humble spirits, for God gives special blessings to those who are humble" (1 Pet. 5:5, *TLB*).

I'll go where you want me to go, dear Lord,
real service is what I desire.
I'll sing a solo any time, dear Lord,
but don't ask me to sing in the choir.

I'll do what you want me to do, dear Lord,
I like to see things come to pass.
But don't ask me to teach boys and girls, O
        Lord.
I'd rather just stay in my class.

I'll do what you want me to do, dear Lord,
I yearn for Thy kingdom to thrive.
I'll give you my nickels and dimes, dear Lord.
But please don't ask me to tithe.[3]

There are some prices to be paid for servant-leadership.

My friend Joyce is a choir director in her middle-size church. (Her name has been changed to protect the innocent.) We were having lunch together and talking over this book and some of her great ideas for her expanding choir program for the fall.

"Be sure to tell some of the things a servant-leader is not allowed to do. I have learned some of them the hard way. Some might just be for choir directors, but perhaps they apply to any leadership position." Here goes:

1. The leader is not allowed to have excuses, like headaches, dentist appointments, or lack of funds.

2. The leader is not allowed to have birthday celebrations or anniversaries that land on choir practice nights.

3. The leader is not allowed to attend her children's program at school if it conflicts with anything having to do with the choir. (Half the choir can leave after going over the Introit twice for next Sunday in order to be on time to see the school awards program—but *the director must stay at her post!*)

4. The leader is not allowed to disagree with anyone who has a better suggestion.

5. The leader is not allowed to be disgusted or to react either violently—or occasionally even non-violently—to a lack of courtesy on the part of the lead-ees.

Does it sound familiar at all? Dragging yourself to a rehearsal or a meeting feeling like you have one foot in the grave yourself, and the phone rings again; Bertha just cannot make it—and she was to bring the refreshments. The leader must always have something in the freezer!

Don't you sometimes wonder that we have any leaders at all in our churches?

Let's hurry on then, to some examples of service in the Word and then to the servant's reward.

It was in the upper room. Peter reacted to Jesus' suggestion that He wanted to wash Peter's dusty feet. Did each of those disciples hope that one of the others would take care of this customary amenity? Did John say, under his breath, "Let James do it—I am tired." Or did Nathanael give that look across the room that spoke louder than any words, indicating that it was about time Matthew got down off his high horse and started serving?

However it happened, it was Jesus Himself who took the basin and towel and served.

· "I have set you an example that you should do as I have done for you. . . . No servant is greater than his master. . . . You know these things, you will be blessed if you do them" (John 13:15-17).

If ever there lived one who could have said do as I say, it was the Lord of glory. Instead, He gently exhorted, "do as I do."

It was only the pastor's third Sunday in his new church. He told the worshipers that he had wanted to bring a wash basin and a towel and place it in the front of the sanctuary by the pulpit. But he could only find a chipped enamel bowl in the kitchen, and a kitchen towel in the front of the church might raise a few eyebrows, so he decided against it.

"Besides," he said, "if I had done with that basin and towel what Jesus did, we would have all felt a little uncomfortable. If I were to have gone down to you high school boys on the third row and asked you to take off your shoes so that I could wash your feet, I am not sure which of us would have been the *most* uncomfortable— you or me. Perhaps that same hesitancy is felt as we move out into the daily-ness of our lives between Sundays, in our service. Many of us feel inept at a basin and towel, whether we are being served, or are serving in humility."

He confronted the congregation with the strong words of Jesus, do as I do! None of us left that service, I am certain, without the conviction of the Spirit of God upon us to become servants, with a basin-and-towel ministry.

Our family was traveling together. I find that the hours spent in the car give time for talking, sleeping, listening to tapes, and also reading a good book together. When we were leaving for California I picked off the shelf, before the movers came for the boxes and crates, the classic by Charles Sheldon, *In His Steps*. We managed to finish it just before crossing the Oakland Bay Bridge!

Nearly one hundred years ago Sheldon wrote this book—a novel—as a series of sermons. Since the lessons still need to be learned, the book has survived into this time, with many, many printings.

A town was suffering unemployment, a skid row blight on its inner city, breaking hearts behind high society's doors, and creating apathy in the church. A stranger's substitute sermon on the topic, "What Would Jesus Do?" became a challenge acted on by several members of the congregation. Those four words became a commitment to a changing life-style. And the story line is the unfolding of the effects on the town, its businesses and its people by the simple application and forethought of what Christ Himself would have done in any given situation.

There is so much in the Scripture that lets us know what Jesus would do. Jesus would not defend His own reputation when criticized unjustly; Jesus would not waste time and energy in self-justification, or take popularity polls about His leadership. Jesus would not harbor resentment when others disappointed Him; Jesus would not indulge in comparisons about levels of commitment.

"Your attitude should be the same as that of Christ Jesus; Who, being in very nature God, did not consider equality with God something to be grasped, but made himself nothing, taking the very nature of a servant, being made in human likeness" (Phil. 2:5-7).

> Take my will and make it thine;
> it shall be no longer mine.
> Take my heart, it is thine own;
> it shall be thy royal throne.[4]

Another example is Philip. In the book of Acts we read that some changes had to be made organizationally in the fellowship of believers. There was some complaining by the Grecian Jews against the native Hebrews that their widows were not being given their rightful supply of food. So a committee meeting was held, and a serving committee was chosen. These were to be waiters—servants—and the qualifications were high for waiting on tables! They were to be full of the Spirit of God and wisdom.

Is this not in keeping with the scriptural principles of greatness and leadership?

"Whoever Wishes to Be Great" is the title of an article by Dr. Howard Hendricks for *Worldwide Challenge* magazine. He gives this insight: "Philip, the great evangelist, also got his start serving tables. Perhaps it was his experience in serving people that made him sensitive to the voice of God. When the Spirit came to him in Samaria, telling him to go down into the desert, Philip didn't say, 'Lord, I'm a metropolitan man, I've got a big city-wide campaign going here. I don't specialize in those desert experiences.'

"He knew that if God were calling the shots, he couldn't lose. And it is altogether possible that the Ethiopian he led to Christ became the man who opened the whole continent of Africa to the gospel in the first century.

"My friends, you shouldn't gripe if God has you serving tables. Who knows, you could be in training for evangelism. God could have you serving tables now to prepare you for a far greater ministry later."[5]

Jesus had something to say about serving tables back in the book of Luke. "For who is greater, the one who is at the table or the one who serves? Is it not the one who is at the table? But I am among you as one who serves" (22:27). Then He goes on to let us in on a part of the reward for servants:

"I confer on you a kingdom, just as my Father conferred one on me, so that you may eat and drink at my table in my kingdom and sit on thrones" (22:29,30).

I for one don't want to miss it! Hand me my basin and towel, or my tray and apron!

There is another kind of reward for service pictured in

Matthew in the parable of the talents. Do you remember that the talents were distributed, and the one with the least dug a hole and buried his. The next invested his and gained five more. But the one to whom the most was given did well! He made the biggest investment and realized the most returns for the Master. So, what was his reward? A vacation? A bonus? NO!

*More work*, more responsibility, a wider sphere of service.

"You have been faithful with a few things; I will put you in charge of many things" (Matt. 25:21). Can that be translated, "You have done so well with the visiting plan for this nursing home, I will allow you to coordinate the schedule and program for all five that our church is responsible for each month"? Or "How well you have been working on the kitchen committee; so that you know where everything is, now you can plan the annual women's luncheon for 300 in May!"

Count on it—God has more for you in mind.

> Take my love; my Lord, I pour at thy feet its
> treasure store;
> Take myself, and I will be ever, only, all for
> Thee.[6]

Then as you acquire poise as a speaker-teacher:
● learn the techniques of recruiting others as a leader-soldier;
● practice coaching others and setting higher goals as a coach-athlete;
● grow up into Christ yourself and learn to encourage growth in others as a leader-farmer;
● work hard to build the Word of God into every life you enter as a workman-builder;
● intercede as a vessel-leader set apart for Spirit-filled service, then—*you will be a servant*.

Women, sharpen your skills, reach out to embrace

new opportunities for service. Present yourselves to the Lord for service. Volunteer to lead. Is it enough for you to look forward to the "Well done, thou good and faithful servant" as your glorious reward?

## Notes

1. Author unknown.
2. Frances R. Havergal, "Take My Life."
3. Author unknown.
4. Havergal, "Take My Life."
5. Howard Hendricks, "Whoever Wishes to Be Great," *Worldwide Challenge.*
6. Havergal, "Take My Life."